N8N AI in Action

Automate Smart Workflows with Ease

Written By

Charles Sprinter

Table of Content

Chapter 1: Introduction to n8n and AI Automation

1.1 What is n8n?

n8n (short for *"nodemation"*) is an open-source, low-code automation platform that lets you connect apps, services, and custom code to build powerful workflows — visually.

Think of it as a **developer-friendly alternative to Zapier**, but with more flexibility, self-hosting options, and built-in support for **JavaScript, APIs, and logic customization**.

✅ **Key Features of n8n:**

Feature	Description
□ Node-based workflow editor	Drag-and-drop interface to chain operations visually
🔌 350+ integrations	Supports APIs like Slack, OpenAI, Gmail, Notion, PostgreSQL, etc.
□ Built-in AI support	Native nodes for OpenAI and Hugging Face
💻 Custom code nodes	Add custom JS logic directly into your workflows
🚀 Self-hosting friendly	Can run on your own server, cloud, Docker, or even Raspberry Pi
🔐 Secure credentials	Built-in credential management to connect APIs safely

□ Why Should Developers Care?

n8n gives you the **power of a full backend automation engine** — without needing to write an entire backend service from scratch.

You can:

- Automate tasks across tools (e.g., auto-reply to emails, enrich customer data)
- Trigger actions via webhooks, schedules, or events
- Integrate **AI services** like OpenAI to make workflows intelligent

---

□ Real-World Example:

Let's say you're a dev building a support system. With n8n, you can:

1. Trigger a workflow when a support ticket is submitted via Typeform.
2. Use OpenAI to summarize or tag the ticket automatically.
3. Store the processed data into Airtable.
4. Notify the support team in Slack — all without writing a backend.

⚙□ Behind the Scenes (How n8n Works):

Workflows in n8n are made up of **nodes**. Each node does one task:

- A trigger node starts the workflow (e.g., a new form submission).
- Operation nodes process data (e.g., call OpenAI).
- Output nodes send results somewhere (e.g., email, Slack, DB).

Here's a simple **flowchart** of how a typical AI workflow looks in n8n:

```css
[Trigger: New Email] → [OpenAI: Summarize Email] → [Send
Slack Notification]
```

□ Mini Exercise

Goal: Open n8n and create your first simple workflow.

Steps:

1. Open https://cloud.n8n.io or install locally.

2. Create a workflow with:
   - o A `Manual Trigger` node.
   - o A `Set` node to define sample data like:

```json
{
  "message": "Hello, world!"
}
```

   - o A `Webhook Response` node to output the data.
3. Run the workflow.

☐ **Result**: You've just run your first n8n workflow!

1.2 Why n8n for AI-Powered Workflows?

AI tools like OpenAI and Hugging Face are incredibly powerful — but connecting them to real-world use cases often requires backend glue: handling APIs, structuring data, triggering events, storing results, and integrating with other systems.

That's where **n8n** shines. It acts as the **orchestrator** that brings AI into your daily workflows without needing to build custom microservices or write full-blown backend code.

🚀 Benefits of Using n8n for AI Workflows

Feature / Capability	How It Helps with AI Workflows
🔌 Native AI Node Support	Built-in integrations with **OpenAI**, **Hugging Face**, and others
☐ Modular Node System	Chain AI calls with services like Gmail, Notion, Slack, etc.
☐ JavaScript Support	Use `Function` or `Code` nodes to tweak AI prompts or handle model output
☐ Dynamic Data Handling	Fetch, clean, transform, and route data with zero boilerplate

Feature / Capability	How It Helps with AI Workflows
☐ Context-Aware Flows	Maintain memory/context across workflow runs (great for chatbots, pipelines)
💡 Visual Debugging	See exactly how your data flows, making AI output handling easier
☐ No DevOps Overhead	Run in the cloud, self-host, or test locally with Docker

☐ Real Developer Value

Here's what n8n gives you **as an automation engineer or developer** working with AI:

- **Speed**: Prototype AI workflows in minutes
- **Control**: Customize logic with JS and conditionals
- **Extendability**: Connect AI outputs to hundreds of APIs instantly
- **Debuggability**: Spot and fix issues with built-in logs and execution history
- **Self-hosting**: Avoid cloud limitations and control data privacy

☐ Example: From Text to Action

Imagine you want to build a support tool that:

Takes a customer message → summarizes it with GPT → sends it to Slack with proper urgency tags

With n8n, that's just **4 nodes**:

css

```
[Trigger: New Message] → [OpenAI: Summarize + Detect Urgency]
                → [If: High Urgency?] → [Slack: Send
Alert]
```

No backend code, no waiting on a dev team — just plug and play.

⊙ When to Use n8n for AI

Use n8n when you need to:

✓ Automate repetitive tasks using AI (e.g., summarize, translate, extract info)
✓ Build prototypes fast without backend overhead
✓ Connect AI outputs to your databases, emails, or APIs
✓ Chain multiple tools (e.g., OpenAI + Pinecone + Notion)
✓ Host your own flows with privacy control

⚡ Bonus: AI Use Cases n8n Makes Easy

Use Case	Tools Used in n8n Workflow
Smart email replies	Gmail + OpenAI + Delay + Gmail
Content classification	Webhook + Hugging Face + Airtable
AI-powered data enrichment	API + OpenAI + Google Sheets
Sentiment analysis in feedback forms	Typeform + OpenAI + Slack
AI chatbot with memory	Webhook + OpenAI + Notion/Airtable

✓ Summary

n8n is **the missing link** between AI services and real-world systems. It helps you:

- Automate smarter
- Build faster
- Control workflows end-to-end

1.3 Benefits for Automation Engineers & Developers

If you're an **automation engineer** or **developer**, you're probably juggling multiple tools, APIs, and logic chains to build intelligent systems. n8n makes this easier by letting you visually design workflows, integrate AI seamlessly, and inject custom logic where needed — **without writing full backend apps**.

Here's why **n8n is a game-changer** for you:

🔧 1. Visual Workflow Design (But Still Dev-Friendly)

You don't lose power just because it's low-code. With n8n, you:

- Build flows with drag-and-drop nodes.
- Dive into JavaScript wherever needed (via `Function` or `Code` nodes).
- Debug easily using built-in execution logs.

➤ *Think of it as a visual programming language that speaks APIs, AI, and logic.*

⚡ 2. Easy AI Integration Without the Glue Code

Traditionally, using AI like OpenAI or Hugging Face in a backend app involves:

1. Calling the API
2. Handling auth + tokens
3. Cleaning the input
4. Formatting the output
5. Connecting to other services

With n8n:

You drop an **OpenAI node**, paste your prompt, and link the result to the next step. Done.

3. Workflow Reusability & Versioning

As a dev, your workflows are **modular** and **reusable**:

- Shareable JSON templates
- Version control via Git integrations
- Easy export/import across projects or teams

This means you can build once and reapply anywhere.

🔍 4. Built-in Debugging & Data Inspection

Every time a workflow runs, n8n:

- Stores an execution history
- Lets you inspect inputs/outputs of every node
- Makes error tracing simple

💡 No need to console.log anything — it's all visual.

🔐 5. Secure Credential Handling

n8n makes API integration safer:

- Store tokens/keys securely using built-in credential manager
- Use OAuth2 flows where needed
- Keep secrets out of workflows and code

6. Extend with Code Where It Counts

Need logic that's too complex for built-in nodes? Use:

- `Function` nodes to process items with JavaScript
- `HTTP Request` nodes to call any external API
- `Code` nodes for advanced scripting

This lets you build **hybrid solutions** — code where needed, automate the rest.

☐ 7. Prototype → Production in One Tool

Whether you're just testing an AI use case or deploying a live system:

- Start with a manual trigger or webhook
- Add real-time event triggers (e.g., form submissions, email events)
- Schedule workflows for background jobs
- Deploy to cloud or Docker for production

You don't need to move between tools — n8n scales with your needs.

☐ Quick Challenge: Your First Dev-Friendly Flow

Task: Create a simple flow that:

- Uses a `Webhook` node as input
- Sends the input to OpenAI to rewrite the message politely
- Returns the polite message in the response

Try it and check the execution log to see how each node handled the data!

✅ Summary for Engineers & Devs

Problem	n8n Solution
Too much glue code for AI	Drag-and-drop OpenAI / Hugging Face nodes
Hard to debug backend logic	Visual logs + data explorer
Repetitive automation scripts	Reusable and sharable workflows
Managing credentials securely	Built-in credential manager
Building prototypes takes time	One-click deployable visual workflows

n8n empowers you to build **AI-powered, API-connected, event-driven systems** — fast, clean, and with full control.

1.4 Quick Look at Supported AI Tools (OpenAI, Hugging Face, etc.)

n8n makes it easy to add intelligence to your workflows by integrating with popular AI tools — no backend, no glue code, no complicated setup.

Let's take a **quick tour of the top AI tools supported in n8n** and what you can do with them.

☐ 1. OpenAI (GPT Models)

The **OpenAI node** lets you connect directly to GPT models like `gpt-3.5-turbo` or `gpt-4`.

۹ What You Can Do:

- Generate smart replies to emails
- Summarize articles or support tickets
- Extract key information from text
- Translate or rewrite content

☐☐ Node Features:

- Supports `chat` and `completion` models

- Customizable system/user prompts
- Adjustable temperature, max tokens, and stop sequences

□ Example Use Case:

```
n8n

[Trigger: New Support Ticket] → [OpenAI: Summarize + Tag] →
[Notion: Save Summary]
```

□ 2. Hugging Face

n8n also supports **Hugging Face**, a hub for thousands of open-source ML models in NLP, vision, and more.

🔍 What You Can Do:

- Perform sentiment analysis
- Classify text into categories
- Extract named entities
- Use zero-shot classification for tagging content

□□ Node Features:

- Connect via Hugging Face API
- Choose hosted models (e.g., `distilbert-base-uncased`, `facebook/bart-large-mnli`)
- Easily parse results for downstream workflows

□ Example Use Case:

```
n8n

[Trigger: New Form Submission] → [Hugging Face: Sentiment
Analysis] → [Slack: Notify]
```

🎁 3. Custom HTTP Request to Other AI APIs

Even if an AI tool isn't officially integrated yet, n8n lets you call **any AI API** using the `HTTP Request` node.

You can integrate:

- Claude (Anthropic)
- Gemini (Google)
- Mistral
- Cohere
- Replicate (for image/video generation)

As long as the API has a REST interface, you're good to go.

☐ Example Use Case:

```
n8n

[Webhook: Input Text] → [HTTP Request: Gemini API] → [Set:
Format Result] → [Webhook Response]
```

🔧 4. n8n AI Plugins and Community Nodes

Some community-created nodes also support AI tools like:

- **Stability AI** (image generation)
- **Replicate** (run ML models via API)
- **Whisper** (audio transcription from OpenAI)

You can install these using n8n's **community node manager**.

☐☐ Quick Comparison Table

AI Tool	Main Use Case	Integration Method
OpenAI	Chat, summarization, rewrite	Built-in OpenAI Node
Hugging Face	Sentiment, classification	Built-in Hugging Face Node

AI Tool	Main Use Case	Integration Method
Anthropic	Claude-based chat/completion	HTTP Request
Google Gemini	Search-powered LLM	HTTP Request
Cohere	Embeddings, classification	HTTP Request
Replicate	Image/video ML model execution	HTTP Request / Plugin

✅ Summary

With n8n, you can plug in AI with just a few clicks:

- **Use OpenAI for text generation**
- **Use Hugging Face for smart analysis**
- **Use HTTP Requests for cutting-edge APIs**
- All within one visual workflow — no glue code, no stress.

Chapter 2: Setting Up Your n8n Environment

2.1 Installing n8n Locally and via Docker

Before building AI-powered workflows in n8n, you need a working environment. You can run n8n in two main ways:

1. **Locally on your machine (Node.js setup)**
2. **Using Docker (isolated and portable)**

Let's go through both step by step.

✅ Option 1: Install n8n Locally (Without Docker)

🔧 Prerequisites:

Make sure you have these installed:

- Node.js (v18+ recommended)
- npm
- npx (comes with npm)

▶️ Step-by-Step:

1. Create a project folder:

bash

```
mkdir n8n-local
cd n8n-local
```

2. Install n8n:

bash

```
npm install n8n -g
```

3. Run n8n:

bash

n8n

This starts n8n on `http://localhost:5678` by default.

✅ Done!

You can now open your browser and start building workflows at:
http://localhost:5678

🐳 Option 2: Install n8n via Docker (Recommended for Stability)

Docker gives you an isolated, production-like environment — perfect for testing real-world workflows with external APIs like OpenAI.

🔧 Prerequisites:

- Docker installed
- Docker Compose

▶️ Step-by-Step: Docker Setup

1. Create a new directory:

bash

```
mkdir n8n-docker
cd n8n-docker
```

2. Create a `docker-compose.yml` file:

yaml

```yaml
version: '3.7'

services:
  n8n:
    image: n8nio/n8n
    restart: always
    ports:
      - "5678:5678"
    environment:
      - N8N_BASIC_AUTH_ACTIVE=true
      - N8N_BASIC_AUTH_USER=admin
      - N8N_BASIC_AUTH_PASSWORD=securepassword
      - N8N_HOST=localhost
      - N8N_PORT=5678
      - NODE_ENV=production
    volumes:
      - ./n8n_data:/home/node/.n8n
```

💡 **Pro Tip**: This also sets up basic auth so random users can't access your instance.

3. Start the container:

```bash
bash

docker-compose up -d
```

4. Access the instance:

Open your browser to
http://localhost:5678
Log in with the username and password you set in the `.env` or `docker-compose.yml`.

☐ Test it Works

Once running, try this:

1. Create a new workflow.
2. Add a **Manual Trigger** node.
3. Add a **Set** node and define sample output like:

    ```json
    json
    ```

```
{
    "message": "Hello from local n8n!"
}
```

4. Click **Execute Workflow** to run it.

✅ If you see the message, your setup is working!

📌 Summary Table

Method	Pros	Best For
Local (Node.js)	Simple setup, fast testing	Beginners, dev environments
Docker	Isolated, secure, production-like	Devs, teams, production-ready

2.2 Setting Up a Free Cloud Workspace (e.g., n8n Cloud or Free-Tier Hosting)

Not ready to install n8n locally or run Docker? No worries. You can start building AI-powered workflows right away using **n8n Cloud** or free hosting platforms like **Render**, **Railway**, or **Fly.io**.

Let's look at the easiest and fastest option first.

☁️ Option 1: Using n8n Cloud (Official Cloud Hosting)

n8n Cloud is the official hosted version of n8n, managed by the n8n team. It takes care of hosting, security, updates, and lets you focus on building workflows.

🚀 Features:

- No setup required
- Fastest way to get started
- Comes with credential storage
- Includes the OpenAI node out of the box
- Free trial available (14 days)

▶️ Step-by-Step:

1. Go to https://cloud.n8n.io
2. Click **"Start Free Trial"**
3. Sign up with email or GitHub/Google
4. You'll be taken to your personal n8n workspace
5. Start creating workflows immediately!

☐ **Tip**: You can run up to **200 executions per day** during the trial — perfect for testing AI workflows.

FREE Option 2: Free-Tier Self-Hosting (For More Control)

Want more flexibility or to host your own instance for free? You can deploy n8n on free cloud platforms like:

◆ Render.com (Free Tier)

1. Go to https://render.com
2. Create a free account
3. Click **"New Web Service"** and link your GitHub repo with n8n
4. Use this example repo: https://github.com/n8n-io/n8n
5. Set environment variables:
   - `N8N_BASIC_AUTH_USER`
   - `N8N_BASIC_AUTH_PASSWORD`
   - `WEBHOOK_URL` (set to your public URL)
6. Choose free tier and deploy

☐ You'll get a public URL like:
`https://n8n-yourapp.onrender.com`

◆ Railway.app (Fastest Dev Deploy)

1. Visit https://railway.app
2. Sign in and click **"New Project"** → **"Deploy from GitHub repo"**
3. Use the `n8n-io/n8n` repo
4. Set up the environment like with Render
5. Click **Deploy**

✅ You now have a free n8n instance with 500 hours of runtime/month.

◆ Fly.io (For Global Hosting)

1. Install flyctl
2. Run:

```bash
fly launch
```

3. Choose an app name and region
4. Configure environment
5. Deploy using:

```bash
fly deploy
```

⚙☐ **Pro tip**: Use Fly.io if you need low-latency AI workflows hosted close to your users.

📌 Summary Table: Cloud Options

Platform	Setup Time	Free Tier Highlights	Best For
n8n Cloud	⏱ 1 min	14-day free trial, no config needed	Beginners, fast testing
Render	⏱ 5 mins	Free web service with env vars	Small production workflows
Railway	⏱ 3 mins	500 free hours/month	Devs prototyping fast
Fly.io	⏱ 10 mins	Free CPU credits, global hosting	Advanced, low-latency needs

☐ Quick Exercise: Set Up Your Cloud n8n Instance

Try either:

- **Option A**: Sign up for n8n Cloud and create a workflow with a Manual Trigger.
- **Option B**: Deploy to Render and test an HTTP Webhook workflow.

✓☐ Either method gives you a ready-to-use cloud workspace for building AI-powered flows in the next chapters.

2.3 Connecting APIs and Credentials Securely

To build real-world, AI-powered workflows in n8n, you'll often need to connect external services like:

- OpenAI (for GPT prompts)
- Hugging Face (for text classification)
- Notion, Slack, Gmail, Airtable, and others

n8n makes credential handling easy and secure with a **built-in credential manager**.

🔐 Why Secure Credentials Matter

You never want to hardcode API keys or secrets directly into workflows — it's insecure, error-prone, and hard to update.

n8n solves this by letting you:

- Store secrets in a secure vault
- Reuse credentials across nodes
- Avoid leaking keys in workflow exports or shared templates

🔧 How to Add Credentials in n8n

Let's walk through how to safely connect an API like OpenAI:

✅ Step-by-Step: Connect to OpenAI

1. Open a workflow and add an OpenAI Node

- Click the node → Go to the **"Credentials"** field
- Click **"Create New"**

2. In the credential dialog:

- Give it a name (e.g., `my-openai-key`)
- Paste your **OpenAI API Key** (from https://platform.openai.com/account/api-keys)

3. Click Save

🔐 This credential is now securely stored — it can only be used by authorized nodes in this n8n instance.

☐ Pro Tip: If you're self-hosting, credentials are encrypted and stored in your `.n8n` directory. Protect this with proper file permissions and backups.

☐ Reusing Credentials Across Workflows

Once you've created a credential, you can:

- Select it in any new node that supports the same service
- Manage it globally via the **Credentials tab** in the main menu
- Easily revoke or update keys without editing every node

This saves time and keeps your secrets centralized.

⚙☐ Supported Auth Methods in n8n

Auth Type	Description	Examples
API Key	Most common method for AI services	OpenAI, Hugging Face, Gemini
OAuth2	For apps that require login + token exchange	Google, Slack, Notion, GitHub
Basic Auth	Username + password	HTTP APIs, internal tools
Custom Headers	Manually set Authorization or Bearer tokens	Any RESTful service

☐ Updating or Revoking Credentials

1. Go to **Credentials** tab in the n8n sidebar
2. Click the credential you want to update
3. Make changes (e.g., paste a new token)
4. Save and test

☛☐ Updating the credential here automatically updates **all workflows** that use it.

25

🚨 Best Practices for Secure API Use

Practice	Why It Matters
Use environment variables	Great for Docker/cloud to avoid hardcoding secrets
Don't expose credentials in logs	AI nodes may return sensitive outputs
Rotate API keys regularly	Limits risk from compromised keys
Use OAuth where possible	Safer than static API keys for some integrations
Restrict API scopes	Only give permissions needed for your workflow

🔲 Quick Exercise: Connect to OpenAI and Test

1. Go to https://platform.openai.com/account/api-keys
2. Copy your API key
3. Create a new workflow with:
   - A `Manual Trigger` node
   - An `OpenAI` node using your new credential
   - A prompt like:
     "Rewrite this sentence to sound more formal: Hello, I need your help."
4. Run the workflow

✅ If you get a response, your connection is secure and successful!

✅ Recap

- Use n8n's **Credential Manager** to safely store and manage API keys
- Avoid hardcoding credentials in workflows

- Support for OpenAI, Hugging Face, and 350+ other services is built-in
- Reuse credentials across nodes and workflows easily

Chapter 3: Getting Started with AI Nodes

3.1 Overview of Built-In AI Nodes

n8n comes with built-in support for major AI platforms, allowing you to add intelligent capabilities like text generation, classification, translation, summarization, and more — all without writing complex backend code.

AI nodes in n8n work just like other nodes: you pass in data, configure the node, and use the result downstream in your workflow.

🔍 Built-In AI Nodes in n8n

Here are the most commonly used built-in AI nodes available in n8n:

☐ 1. OpenAI Node

The OpenAI node lets you use GPT models (gpt-3.5-turbo, gpt-4, etc.) to perform:

- Chat completions
- Text rewriting
- Summarization
- Classification
- Translation

Key Options:

- **Model Selection**: Choose the model (gpt-3.5, gpt-4)
- **System Prompt**: Set instructions (e.g., "You are a helpful assistant.")
- **User Input**: Dynamically pass text from previous nodes
- **Max Tokens & Temperature**: Control output length and creativity

☑ *Best for general-purpose text generation and language tasks.*

☐ 2. Hugging Face Node

This node connects to **Hugging Face Inference API**, where you can use models for:

- Sentiment analysis
- Zero-shot classification
- Named entity recognition
- Summarization and translation (via T5, BART, etc.)

Key Options:

- **Model ID**: e.g., `distilbert-base-uncased-finetuned-sst-2-english`
- **Task Type**: e.g., `text-classification`, `zero-shot-classification`
- **Inputs**: Send text input from previous nodes
- **Parameters**: Optional tweaks to inference behavior

☑ *Best for NLP tasks with fine-tuned or custom models.*

🔧 3. AI via HTTP Request Node (Custom)

While not an "AI" node per se, the `HTTP Request` node is often used to connect with **non-native AI services**, such as:

- **Anthropic Claude**
- **Google Gemini (via PaLM API)**
- **Mistral**
- **Cohere**
- **Replicate (for ML models like image generation)**

You simply send a POST request to the API endpoint and handle the response like any other data.

✅ *Best for using newer or less common LLM APIs.*

🎨 4. Community/Plugin AI Nodes

Using n8n's **community node system**, you can install additional nodes for:

- **Stability AI** (image generation)
- **Replicate** (run almost any Hugging Face or custom model)
- **Whisper API** (audio transcription with OpenAI)

Installation example:

```bash
n8n-nodes-stabilityai
```

✅ *Great for niche or creative AI use cases (audio, images, etc.).*

⚙️ How AI Nodes Fit in Your Workflow

AI nodes typically sit **in the middle** of a workflow. You feed in data from a trigger or API, process it with an AI node, then route the output.

Sample Flow:

```n8n
[Webhook: Incoming Message]
   ↓
[OpenAI: Summarize + Detect Intent]
   ↓
[If: Is Urgent?]
   ↓
[Slack: Alert Team] → [Notion: Save Summary]
```

The AI node acts as a **"smart processor"** between input and action.

☐ Quick Hands-On Exercise

Goal: Use OpenAI to rewrite a message politely.

Steps:

1. Create a new workflow.
2. Add a **Manual Trigger**.
3. Add an **OpenAI Node**:
   - o   Model: `gpt-3.5-turbo`
   - o   System prompt: "You are a polite assistant."
   - o   User message: "Send the report ASAP!"
4. Add a **Set** node to view the AI output.
5. Run the workflow.

✅ Output: You'll get a rewritten message like
"Could you please send the report at your earliest convenience?"

📌 Summary

Node	Use Case	Best For
OpenAI	Chat, rewrite, summarize, classify	General AI tasks
Hugging Face	Sentiment, NER, custom NLP	Specific NLP models
HTTP Request	Claude, Gemini, Mistral, Replicate	Custom or cutting-edge AI APIs
Community Nodes	Image/audio generation, niche models	Creative or non-text AI tasks

3.2 Using the OpenAI Node for Prompt-Response Workflows

The **OpenAI node** in n8n lets you generate smart responses, summaries, rewrites, or even perform classification tasks — all by sending prompts to models like `gpt-3.5-turbo` or `gpt-4`.

Let's walk through how it works and how to build practical prompt-response workflows with it.

💡 What Is a Prompt-Response Workflow?

It's a flow where you:

1. Trigger an input (e.g., a message, form, or email)
2. Send that input to OpenAI with a custom prompt
3. Use the AI-generated response to take an action (e.g., send a reply, tag data, store a result)

▢ Anatomy of the OpenAI Node

When you add an OpenAI node in n8n, you configure:

Field	Description
Model	Choose `gpt-3.5-turbo`, `gpt-4`, etc.
System Message	Set the AI's behavior (e.g., "You are a helpful assistant")
User Message	The input text you want the AI to respond to (can be dynamic)
Temperature	Controls creativity (lower = more predictable)
Max Tokens	Controls how long the output can be
Response Property	Choose how to return the AI's response (default: `message`)

▢▢ Step-by-Step: Build a Prompt-Response Workflow

Let's build a basic OpenAI-powered workflow that rewrites messages politely.

▶□ Step 1: Add a Manual Trigger

- Drag in a **Manual Trigger** node to test your workflow manually.

▶□ Step 2: Add a Set Node (Sample Input)

- Add a **Set** node and define this sample input:

```json
json

{
  "message": "Send me the report ASAP!"
}
```

- Click **"Add Value"** → **"String"** and name it `message`.

▶□ Step 3: Add the OpenAI Node

- Add the **OpenAI** node.
- Connect your OpenAI credentials (see Chapter 2.3).
- Select `gpt-3.5-turbo` as the model.
- In **System Message**, type:

```css
css

You are a polite assistant. Rephrase user input to be
more formal.
```

- In **User Message**, type:

```bash
bash

{{$json["message"]}}
```

This dynamically pulls input from the previous node.

▶☐ Step 4: View the Output

- Add a **Set** or **Webhook Response** node to view the result.
- The OpenAI response will be in `{{$json["message"]}}`.

▶☐ Step 5: Execute the Workflow

Click **Execute Workflow** — and watch your message become:

"Could you please send me the report at your earliest convenience?"

✅ Success! You've built your first AI prompt-response flow.

☐ Common Use Cases

Use Case	System Message Example
Summarize support tickets	"Summarize the following issue in 1-2 sentences."
Translate content	"Translate this text to French."
Rewrite professionally	"Rewrite this message in a formal tone."
Extract info	"Extract the order number and delivery address from the message."
Classify messages	"Classify the message as billing, technical support, or feedback."

☐ Try It Yourself

Change the `System Message` and `User Message` to experiment:

```yaml
System: "You are a creative copywriter. Rewrite the message
to make it catchy."
User: {{$json["message"]}}
```

💡 Pro tip: Use `If` nodes after OpenAI to make decisions based on output (e.g., if sentiment is negative → alert support).

✅ Recap

- The OpenAI node in n8n is your gateway to powerful prompt-response workflows.
- It supports GPT-3.5, GPT-4, and lets you fully customize prompts.
- Combine it with other nodes (like Webhooks, Slack, Notion) to build intelligent flows end-to-end.

3.3 Integrating Hugging Face Models

Hugging Face is one of the largest repositories of machine learning models, especially in **Natural Language Processing (NLP)**. With n8n's built-in Hugging Face node, you can access pre-trained models and easily integrate them into your automation workflows — no need for deep ML knowledge.

▢ What You Can Do with Hugging Face in n8n

Task	Example Output	Model Type
Sentiment Analysis	"positive", "negative", "neutral"	text-classification
Text Classification	"support", "billing", "feedback"	zero-shot-classification
Named Entity Recognition (NER)	Extract names, dates, organizations	token-classification
Summarization	Short summary of a long article	summarization
Translation	English → French, Spanish → English, etc.	translation

🔧 Step-by-Step: Setup Hugging Face in n8n

▶□ Step 1: Get a Hugging Face API Key

1. Go to https://huggingface.co/settings/tokens
2. Click **"New Token"**
3. Copy your **read access** token

▶□ Step 2: Create Hugging Face Credential in n8n

1. Go to **Credentials → Hugging Face API**
2. Click **"Create New"**
3. Paste your token and save

✅ Now you're ready to use the Hugging Face node.

□□ Build an NLP Workflow: Sentiment Analyzer

Let's build a simple workflow that classifies the tone of customer feedback.

□ Workflow Flowchart:

```csharp

[Webhook: New Feedback]
    ↓
[Hugging Face: Sentiment Analysis]
    ↓
[If: Negative?]
    ↓
[Slack: Notify Support Team]
```

▶□ Step-by-Step:

1. Add a Webhook Node

- Set method to POST
- This will receive customer feedback as JSON

2. Add a Hugging Face Node

- Select your Hugging Face credential
- Task: text-classification
- Model: distilbert-base-uncased-finetuned-sst-2-english
- Input: {{$json["feedback"]}}

This model returns sentiment like "POSITIVE" or "NEGATIVE"

3. Add an If Node

- Condition: If {{$json["label"]}} == "NEGATIVE"

4. Add a Slack or Email Node

- Notify the support team if feedback is negative

□ Sample Input:

json

```
{
  "feedback": "I'm very disappointed with the delivery
service."
}
```

✅ Sample Output from Hugging Face:

json

```
[
  {
    "label": "NEGATIVE",
    "score": 0.9823
  }
]
```

☐ Other Hugging Face Use Cases

Task	Suggested Model	Notes
Zero-shot classification	`facebook/bart-large-mnli`	Classify without needing fine-tuning
NER	`dslim/bert-base-NER`	Extract entities like names, dates
Summarization	`facebook/bart-large-cnn`	Works well for long text
Translation	`Helsinki-NLP/opus-mt-en-fr`	English to French

☐ Pro Tip: Combine Hugging Face with OpenAI

Use Hugging Face to detect sentiment or extract keywords, then:

- Feed the result into an **OpenAI node** to generate a reply
- Log insights into Notion or Airtable

Example hybrid flow:

```css
[Webhook Input] → [Hugging Face: Sentiment] → [OpenAI:
Compose Response] → [Send Email]
```

✅ Recap

- Hugging Face in n8n lets you add powerful NLP to your workflows.
- Use pre-trained models for tasks like classification, NER, translation, and more.
- Easy setup via API key + built-in node.
- Combine with OpenAI or other nodes for smarter automations.

Chapter 3: Getting Started with AI Nodes

3.4 AI vs Non-AI Automation: What Changes?

Traditional (non-AI) automation in n8n is all about **clear rules and repeatable logic** — "if X happens, do Y."
AI-powered automation introduces **intelligence and unpredictability**, letting you automate tasks that require human-like thinking: summarizing, translating, classifying, or generating content.

But with great power comes new design decisions.

Let's break it down.

🔍 Traditional Automation in n8n

Feature	Description
Rule-Based	You define exact conditions, paths, and outputs
Deterministic	Same input → same output every time
Fast & Reliable	Runs quickly, minimal variability
Examples	Send email on form submission, update a record, sync CRM data

---

☐ AI-Powered Automation in n8n

Feature	Description
Prompt-Based Logic	Output depends on how you design your prompt and input text
Probabilistic Output	Same input may give slightly different results each time
Language-Driven	Works best for tasks involving text, tone, understanding, or creativity

Feature	Description
Examples	Summarize text, generate email replies, classify sentiment, translate

☐ What Changes for Developers?

Area	Traditional Workflows	AI-Powered Workflows
Input Validation	Strict: if a field is missing → error	Looser: AI can often "guess" missing context
Testing	Unit tests or path-based checks	Need prompt testing, edge case handling
Output Consistency	Always the same	Varies depending on model temperature, prompt
Error Handling	Focus on logic errors	Must handle AI hallucinations or incomplete outputs
Prompt Engineering	Not needed	Critical for quality AI results
Workflow Design	Linear, logic-driven	More dynamic, human-like processing

☐ Example Comparison

💼 Traditional Use Case:

Trigger an email when a user submits a form

Workflow:

```css
[Trigger: New Form Entry] → [Send Email]
```

☐ AI Use Case:

Summarize the user's message and reply politely

Workflow:

```css
[Trigger: New Form Entry] → [OpenAI: Summarize] → [OpenAI:
Generate Reply] → [Send Email]
```

🔍 Notice how the AI workflow:

- Uses **text understanding** instead of static fields
- May need extra **safeguards** to check for bad output
- Offers more power — but also more unpredictability

📌 Best Practices for AI Automation in n8n

Tip	Why It Helps
✅ Set temperature to 0.2–0.5	Makes outputs more consistent
☐ Test prompts with real data	Helps you avoid hallucination or vague responses
🖊 Add fallback logic	If AI fails → send default message or log the issue
☐ Use "If" nodes to validate output	Check for key phrases, categories, or empty responses
🔐 Monitor API usage	AI nodes may consume tokens/cost — set limits if needed

---

⚠️ Important: Know When Not to Use AI

AI is great, but sometimes traditional logic is the better fit.

Don't use AI when:

- The task requires **exact values** (e.g., tax calculations)

- Output must be **legally precise or regulated**
- You need **predictable and fast** processing at scale

💡 Use a **hybrid approach**: combine AI where needed, fall back to logic for critical paths.

✅ Recap

AI Brings...	But Requires...
Intelligence & flexibility	Careful prompt design
Human-like understanding	Output validation and testing
Rich content generation	Fallbacks and guardrails

Understanding these trade-offs helps you **design better, safer AI workflows** that go beyond basic automation.

Chapter 4: Project 1 – Smart Email Reply Generator

4.1 Auto-Replying to Emails Using OpenAI

Goal: Automatically generate and send polite, professional replies to incoming emails using OpenAI and n8n.

This is one of the most practical use cases for combining AI with workflow automation: handling support queries, inquiries, or internal comms — fast and with minimal manual effort.

☐ What You'll Build

A workflow that:

1. Monitors incoming emails (via IMAP or Gmail)
2. Uses OpenAI to generate a polite reply based on the original email
3. Sends the response back automatically

☐ Tools Needed

Tool	Purpose
Email Node	Trigger workflow on incoming email
OpenAI Node	Generate the reply text
Email Node	Send the AI-generated reply
Set Node	Format prompt or message variables

▢▢ Step-by-Step Walkthrough

▶▢ Step 1: Add an Email Trigger

Use the **IMAP Email node** or **Gmail node** to watch for new emails.

- Host: `imap.gmail.com`
- Port: `993`
- Secure: `true`
- Credentials: Use Gmail App Password or OAuth2
- Folder: `INBOX`

▢ *Use a filtered email address or folder if you want to target specific messages (like support@yourdomain.com).*

▶▢ Step 2: Extract Email Content

Add a **Set Node** to extract and simplify fields:

```json
{
  "from": {{$json["from"]["text"]}},
  "subject": {{$json["subject"]}},
  "body": {{$json["text"]}}
}
```

Name this node `Prepare Input`.

▶▢ Step 3: Add OpenAI Node (Generate Reply)

- Model: `gpt-3.5-turbo`
- System Message:

```
css
```

You are a professional assistant. Generate a polite and helpful email reply based on the incoming message.

- User Message:

```
bash
```

```
Subject: {{$json["subject"]}}

Message: {{$json["body"]}}
```

📌 Output will be a generated text reply ready to send.

▶️ Step 4: Send the Reply Email

Add another **Email node** (or Gmail Send node).

- To: {{$json["from"]}}
- Subject: Re: {{$json["subject"]}}
- Body: {{$json["message"]}} *(OpenAI output)*

☐ Add a note or signature if needed — you can append it to the AI output in a **Set** node.

☐ Example Input

Incoming Email:

```
vbnet
```

```
Subject: Need Help with My Order

Hi, I received the wrong item in my package. Can you help me fix this?
```

OpenAI Output:

```
pgsql

Hi there,

Thank you for reaching out. I'm sorry to hear about the mix-
up with your order.

Could you please share your order number so I can assist you
further?

Best regards,
Support Team
```

✅ n8n sends this reply automatically.

☐ Optional: Add Delay + Tagging

Want to avoid instant responses or keep a log?

- Add a **Delay Node** (e.g., wait 5 minutes before replying)
- Add a **Notion / Airtable Node** to log the request and AI response

---

🔐 Best Practices

Tip	Why It Helps
Use filters or folders	Avoid replying to all inbox messages
Log AI replies	For audit trails or human review
Add disclaimers if needed	Let users know it's an AI-generated response
Keep system prompts specific	Improves tone and accuracy of replies
Add retry logic	Handle OpenAI API rate limits or failures

✅ Recap

You just built an AI-powered email assistant that:

- Listens for incoming messages
- Writes a polite, human-like response
- Sends it back instantly

You can expand it with logs, human-in-the-loop steps, or context from previous threads.

4.2 Using Gmail/IMAP + AI + Delay Nodes

In this section, you'll enhance your auto-reply workflow using:

- **Gmail or IMAP** for fetching emails
- **OpenAI** to generate smart responses
- **Delay** nodes to pause responses (e.g., simulate human reply time)

This creates a more realistic and controlled experience for the user and gives you room to inspect or cancel a reply if needed.

☐ Why Add a Delay?

Benefit	Reason
⏱ Avoid instant replies	Makes AI-generated replies feel more human
☐ Rate-limit OpenAI calls	Helps if you're replying to many emails at once
🔍 Time for review (optional)	Allows time to inspect replies manually before sending
⚙☐ Prevent API overload	Especially useful on free or low-tier OpenAI plans

---

☐☐ Step-by-Step: Add Delay to the Email Reply Flow

Let's build on the previous workflow.

▶□ Step 1: Use Gmail or IMAP Trigger

If using Gmail:

- Add the **Gmail Trigger** (OAuth2 required)
- Set it to trigger on **new unread emails**

If using IMAP:

- Add **IMAP Email node**
- Connect to `imap.gmail.com`, port `993`, secure `true`
- Use App Password or OAuth2 to authenticate
- Folder: `INBOX`

▶□ Step 2: Extract Email Data (Set Node)

Extract key fields to use in the prompt:

```json
{
  "from": {{$json["from"]["text"]}},
  "subject": {{$json["subject"]}},
  "body": {{$json["text"]}}
}
```

▶□ Step 3: Add OpenAI Node

Use the same configuration as before:

48

- **System Prompt**:

```css
css
```

```
You are a helpful customer support assistant. Write a
polite reply to the user's message below.
```

- **User Message**:

```bash
bash
```

```
Subject: {{$json["subject"]}}
Body: {{$json["body"]}}
```

The node returns a full, formatted reply in `{{$json["message"]}}`.

▶□ Step 4: Add Delay Node

Insert a **Delay Node** after the OpenAI response and before sending the reply.

Configure Delay Node:

- **Mode**: `Delay For`
- **Time Unit**: `Minutes`
- **Value**: `5`

□ *This tells n8n to wait 5 minutes before sending the email, simulating a natural response time.*

▶□ Step 5: Add Gmail (or SMTP) Send Node

Use the **Gmail Send** or **Email Send** node to send the AI-generated reply:

- To: `{{$json["from"]}}`
- Subject: `Re: {{$json["subject"]}}`
- Body: `{{$json["message"]}}`

✅ Done! Your full AI + delay workflow is complete.

☐ Full Workflow Diagram

```text

[Gmail/IMAP Trigger]
        ↓
   [Set: Extract Email]
        ↓
   [OpenAI: Generate Reply]
        ↓
     [Delay: 5 mins]
        ↓
   [Gmail: Send Reply]
```

☐ Optional Enhancements

Add-On Node	Purpose
☐ "If" Node	Only send replies during work hours
🎁 "Notion / Airtable"	Log replies for record-keeping
👤 "Manual Review"	Use a **Pause** or **approval system** for QA
☐ "Loop / Merge"	Handle batch replies from a folder or tag

✅ Recap

With the **Delay node**, your AI email responder:

- Feels more human
- Avoids API flooding
- Gives you a buffer to review or cancel replies

This setup is great for live environments where user experience and pacing matter.

4.3 Formatting Responses Professionally

OpenAI is powerful, but its responses can sometimes be too long, too casual, or inconsistent in tone. In this section, you'll learn how to:

- Improve the **structure** of replies
- Keep tone consistent and professional
- Use **Set** and **Function** nodes to enhance formatting
- Append signatures or disclaimers

⊙ Why Formatting Matters

Problem	Solution
AI output is too long or vague	Use specific prompt instructions
Tone is inconsistent or too casual	Set tone explicitly in the system prompt
Missing headers or context	Wrap the AI message in standard reply format
You want to add a footer or signature	Use Set node or merge text manually

---

□ Step 1: Refine Your Prompt for Better Output

Modify your **OpenAI system prompt** to encourage clearer, more professional responses.

✍□ Improved System Prompt:

```css
You are a customer support assistant. Respond briefly and
politely in a professional tone. Include a greeting, clear
response, and closing.
```

This ensures a consistent tone like:

"Hi John, thanks for your message. I've forwarded your request to our logistics team. We'll follow up shortly. Best regards, Support Team."

☐ Step 2: Clean Up Output Using a Set Node

After the OpenAI node, insert a **Set Node** to format the final email.

Example:

json

```
{
  "finalReply": "Hi {{$json[\"name\"] ||
'there'}},\n\n{{$json[\"message\"]}}\n\nBest
regards,\nCustomer Support"
}
```

Here:

- `{{$json["message"]}}` is the raw OpenAI output
- You're wrapping it with greeting + sign-off
- Optional: use `"name"` from the email if extracted

🔧 Step 3: Use a Function Node for Advanced Formatting (Optional)

If you want to trim whitespace, convert line breaks, or limit word count, use a `Function` node:

javascript

```
return items.map(item => {
  const raw = item.json.message || "";
  const cleaned = raw.trim().replace(/\n{2,}/g, "\n\n");
  item.json.formatted = `Hi,\n\n${cleaned}\n\nBest
regards,\nSupport Team`;
  return item;
});
```

✉@ Step 4: Use `formatted` Field in Email Node

Now, in your **Send Email** node:

- Body: `{{$json["formatted"]}}`

This ensures only your **professionally structured** response is sent.

📌 Tips for Professional Replies

Tip	How to Do It
Keep tone formal and helpful	Set clear expectations in system prompt
Add greetings + sign-offs	Use Set node or add in prompt
Avoid emojis, slang, or jokes	Instruct OpenAI to "avoid informal language"
Include context if needed	Add subject line or ticket number to user prompt
Wrap replies in HTML (optional)	Use `HTML` content type in Email node for styled replies

---

✉☐ Example: Final Formatted Reply

```
text

Hi Sarah,

Thanks for reaching out. I'm sorry to hear there was an issue
with your delivery.

Could you please share your order number so I can assist
further?

Best regards,
Customer Support
```

✅ This reply is clean, helpful, and ready to be sent in any business context.

✅ Recap

By formatting OpenAI responses:

- You create **trustworthy, client-ready emails**
- Maintain a consistent brand tone
- Avoid awkward or unclear language from the model

Use **prompt tuning**, **Set/Function nodes**, and email formatting to polish your responses before sending them.

Chapter 5: Project 2 – Auto-Tagging Support Tickets

5.1 Pulling in Support Messages from a Source (e.g., Zendesk or Google Sheets)

Goal: Build a workflow that fetches support tickets or messages from a data source like **Zendesk**, **Google Sheets**, or any platform where tickets are logged — so you can tag and route them using AI in the next steps.

🎯 What You'll Learn

- How to connect to external platforms (Zendesk, Sheets)
- How to fetch support messages or tickets
- How to structure the data for AI tagging

🔌 Option 1: Pulling Tickets from Zendesk

n8n includes a built-in **Zendesk node** to fetch tickets via API.

▶️ Step-by-Step (Zendesk):

1. Add the Zendesk Trigger node

- Trigger type: `New Ticket`
- Authenticate with your Zendesk account (API token or OAuth)

📌 Requires Zendesk API access — make sure API is enabled in your settings.

2. Choose fields to pull:

- Subject
- Description

- Requester email
- Priority

3. Optional: Add a Set node to rename fields for clarity:

json

```
{
  "ticket_id": {{$json["id"]}},
  "subject": {{$json["subject"]}},
  "message": {{$json["description"]}}
}
```

✅ You now have the ticket's message and metadata ready for AI processing.

🗒 Option 2: Pulling from Google Sheets

Google Sheets is great for prototyping or when you have manually logged support messages.

▶🗒 Step-by-Step (Google Sheets):

1. Add a Google Sheets node

- Operation: `Read Rows`
- Sheet range: `'SupportTickets'!A2:C100`
  (Assuming columns: `ID, Subject, Message`*)*

📌 Make sure to connect your Google account via OAuth and share the sheet with the connected account.

2. Add a SplitInBatches node (optional)

- Helps process one row at a time
- Set batch size to `1`

3. Use a Set Node to clean up fields:

json

```
{
  "ticket_id": {{$json["ID"]}},
  "subject": {{$json["Subject"]}},
  "message": {{$json["Message"]}}
}
```

✅ You now have a ticket from Sheets ready to pass into OpenAI or Hugging Face for tagging.

☐ Optional Source Ideas

Source Platform	Node Type / Integration
Zendesk	Built-in Zendesk Trigger / Poll
Google Sheets	Google Sheets → Read Rows
Airtable	Airtable → List Records
CSV Upload	Read file via Webhook or Dropbox
Email to Sheet	Use Gmail + Google Sheets

☐ Quick Exercise: Test Input from Google Sheets

1. Add a Google Sheets node → Read a single row
2. Add a Set node → Map fields to `ticket_id`, `subject`, `message`
3. Add a Debug node (or Run Once) to inspect the structure

5.2 Using Sentiment Analysis & Classification

Goal: Automatically analyze support messages to:

- Detect **sentiment** (positive, neutral, negative)
- Classify messages into categories like *billing, technical issue, feature request*, etc.

We'll use **Hugging Face** for sentiment analysis and **OpenAI** (or Hugging Face Zero-Shot models) for category classification.

☐ Why Auto-Tag Support Tickets?

Benefit	Why It Matters
☐ Faster triage	Route tickets to the right team immediately
☐ Context for agents	Help agents prioritize based on urgency or tone
📊 Analytics-ready data	Enables reporting on ticket types and customer mood

🔧 Step-by-Step: Add Sentiment + Category Tags

Let's assume you're getting support tickets from **Google Sheets** or **Zendesk**, and each ticket has a `message` field.

▶☐ Step 1: Add a Hugging Face Node (Sentiment Analysis)

- **Credential**: Select your Hugging Face API key
- **Model**: `distilbert-base-uncased-finetuned-sst-2-english`
- **Task**: `text-classification`
- **Input**: `{{$json["message"]}}`

Sample Output:

```json
[
  {
    "label": "NEGATIVE",
    "score": 0.98
  }
]
```

☐ The `label` field tells us the sentiment — we'll use that as our first tag.

▶☐ Step 2: Add a Set Node to Save Sentiment

json

```
{
  "sentiment": {{$json["label"]}}
}
```

Name this node: `Store Sentiment`.

▶☐ Step 3: Add an OpenAI Node (Category Classification)

- **Model:** `gpt-3.5-turbo`
- **System Prompt:**

  sql

  ```
  You are a support assistant. Read the message and
  return ONLY one category from: Billing, Technical
  Issue, General Question, Feature Request, Complaint.
  ```

- **User Message:**

  bash

  ```
  Message: {{$json["message"]}}
  ```

This ensures OpenAI responds with a **single, consistent category**.

▶☐ Step 4: Add Another Set Node to Store Category

json

```
{
  "category": {{$json["message"]}}
}
```

You now have both:

- `sentiment`: From Hugging Face
- `category`: From OpenAI

☐ Optional: Use Hugging Face for Zero-Shot Classification

Want to avoid using OpenAI? You can also use Hugging Face with zero-shot models.

Model:

- `facebook/bart-large-mnli`

Task:

- `zero-shot-classification`

Candidate Labels:

json

```
["Billing", "Technical Issue", "General Question", "Feature
Request", "Complaint"]
```

✅ Hugging Face will return the **most likely label** based on the message.

☐ Optional: Route Tickets by Tag

Use an **If Node** to route the flow based on tags:

- If `sentiment == "NEGATIVE"` → Alert Support Lead
- If `category == "Billing"` → Send to Finance Queue
- If `category == "Feature Request"` → Log in Notion/Airtable

☐ Sample Message

css

```
Hi, I was charged twice for my subscription and I can't get
through to support.
```

AI Tags Output:

json

```json
{
  "sentiment": "NEGATIVE",
  "category": "Billing"
}
```

✅ You can now log this, alert the billing team, or auto-prioritize based on the tags.

📌 Best Practices

Tip	Why It Helps
Use strict system prompts	Prevents AI from returning vague or multi-category replies
Log tags to a database or spreadsheet	Useful for training future models or dashboards
Add fallback defaults	If no sentiment is detected, default to "Neutral"
Test on real-world ticket samples	Helps validate your prompts and models

✅ Recap

You've now automated:

- Sentiment detection using Hugging Face
- Ticket categorization using OpenAI (or Hugging Face Zero-Shot)
- Structured tags that enable smart routing, analytics, and prioritization

5.3 Auto-Tagging + Writing Summaries

Goal: Automatically:

1. Assign tags to support tickets (like *Billing, Complaint*)
2. Generate a short, helpful summary using OpenAI
3. Store or forward this information for human agents or auto-responses

---

☐ Why Add Summaries?

Benefit	How It Helps
✂☐ Reduces reading time	Agents don't need to read long customer messages
📌 Helps in prioritization	AI summary surfaces critical info first
☐ Powers downstream workflows	Summaries can be reused in replies, logs, and dashboards
💬 Enables consistent context	Great for CRM notes or AI-assisted chat

---

🔧 Step-by-Step: Combine Tagging + Summarization

Let's assume your workflow already has:

- A **support ticket input** (from Zendesk, Google Sheets, etc.)
- A message field (the full ticket content)

- AI-generated **sentiment** and **category**

Now, let's add summarization.

▶□ Step 1: Add OpenAI Node – Summary

Config:

- **Model**: `gpt-3.5-turbo`
- **System Prompt**:

```css
You are a support assistant. Summarize the message in
1-2 sentences. Be concise and professional.
```

- **User Message**:

```bash
Message: {{$json["message"]}}
```

This will output a **summary** of the customer message.

✅ Example Output:

"Customer was charged twice for their subscription and is seeking assistance with a refund."

▶□ Step 2: Use a Set Node to Organize Final Output

Create a final data object to store or pass forward:

```json
{
  "ticket_id": "{{$json["ticket_id"]}}",
  "sentiment": "{{$json["sentiment"]}}",
  "category": "{{$json["category"]}}",
```

```
  "summary": "{{$json["message"]}}"
}
```

✅ Now all AI-generated metadata is combined and structured.

▶️ Step 3: Store or Route the Tagged Summary

You can now:

- **Send to Notion or Airtable** for logging
- **Email a team lead** with the tagged summary
- **Post to Slack** for high-priority cases
- **Auto-assign** using conditional logic based on category

🗂 Full Example Input

Ticket message:

```arduino
I just signed up but got charged twice and didn't get a
confirmation email.
```

🗂 AI Output:

```json
{
  "sentiment": "NEGATIVE",
  "category": "Billing",
  "summary": "User was charged twice after signing up and did
not receive a confirmation email."
}
```

You now have a **quick-to-scan**, **tagged**, and **summarized** ticket for your support team or CRM.

☐ Optional Enhancements

Feature	Node / Technique
✅ Validate AI outputs	Add "If" nodes or default fallbacks
☐ Improve summary quality	Fine-tune prompts for tone/style
🎁 Log results	Store in Google Sheets, Notion, DB
📢 Notify stakeholders	Send summary to Slack or Email node

📌 Workflow Summary

```text
[Trigger: New Ticket]
   ↓
[Set: Extract Fields]
   ↓
[Hugging Face: Sentiment]
   ↓
[OpenAI: Category]
   ↓
[OpenAI: Summary]
   ↓
[Set: Combine Output]
   ↓
[Store or Route: Notion / Slack / CRM]
```

✅ Recap

You now have a complete system that:

- Tags support tickets with **sentiment** and **category**
- Generates concise, human-readable **summaries**
- Routes this enriched data wherever it's needed

This creates faster triage, smarter support, and better customer experiences.

Chapter 6: Project 3 – Intelligent Data Enrichment

6.1 Scraping or Retrieving Raw Data

Goal: Use n8n to fetch raw or unstructured data from external sources — like websites, APIs, CSVs, or emails — so you can clean, enrich, and store it intelligently with the help of AI.

☐ What Is Data Enrichment?

Data enrichment is the process of adding context or value to raw data. In this project, you'll:

- Scrape or retrieve raw content
- Use AI to translate, summarize, categorize, or clean it
- Store the enriched version in a usable format (like a spreadsheet, Notion, or database)

☐☐ Step-by-Step: Retrieving Raw Data

You can collect data from various sources using n8n. Let's look at common options:

☐ Option 1: Scraping Website Content

▶☐ Using HTTP Request Node:

1. Add an **HTTP Request** node
2. Method: GET
3. URL: Any public webpage (e.g., product, blog, profile)

Example:
```
https://example.com/blog/how-to-use-n8n
```

The response will include raw HTML.

▶□ (Optional) Clean HTML with HTML Extract Node:

- Add **HTML Extract** node
- Use a CSS selector to extract specific content
  Example:

  ```
  css
  ```

  ```
  article p
  ```

☑ You now have clean article text to enrich via AI.

□□ Option 2: Reading from CSV or File

▶□ Using Read Binary File + CSV Node:

1. Add a **Read Binary File** node (if file is local or uploaded)
2. Add **CSV node** to parse the data
3. Use **SplitInBatches** node to process one row at a time

Each row can contain product descriptions, leads, feedback — perfect for enrichment.

✉@ Option 3: Extract from Incoming Emails

▶□ Using IMAP Email Node:

1. Connect to your inbox using the IMAP Email node
2. Target a specific folder like `Leads` or `Data`

3. Extract subject/body using a **Set** node

⚡ Option 4: Pull Data from APIs

▶☐ Using HTTP Request Node (API source):

Example: Pull leads from a CRM or article summaries from a blog API

bash

```
GET https://api.example.com/articles?limit=10
```

Authenticate using headers or credentials stored in n8n.

✅ Result: You now have JSON data like:

json

```
{
  "title": "Understanding AI Pipelines",
  "description": "A complete guide to automated AI
workflows..."
}
```

☐ Mini Exercise: Scrape a Blog Post

1. Add an **HTTP Request** node
    URL: `https://example.com/blog-post`
2. Add an **HTML Extract** node
    CSS selector: `article`
3. Add a **Function** node to clean up the content:

javascript

```
return items.map(item => {
  item.json.content = item.json["html"].replace(/<[^>]*>/g,
"").trim();
  return item;
});
```

☑ Output: Clean text ready to enrich in the next section.

📌 Summary Table: Raw Data Sources

Source	Node(s) to Use	Notes
Website	HTTP Request + HTML Extract	Great for articles, product pages
CSV	Read Binary File + CSV + Split	Easy to enrich rows individually
Email	IMAP Email + Set	Extract subject + body
API	HTTP Request	JSON format preferred
Google Sheets	Google Sheets node	Read structured rows for AI

☑ Recap

You now know how to:

- Scrape websites, read files, connect APIs, or pull emails
- Extract and structure raw text for processing
- Prep data for enrichment with OpenAI or Hugging Face

6.2 Using AI for Cleaning, Translation, or Classification

Goal: Transform messy or unstructured data into clean, structured, and usable information using **OpenAI** and **Hugging Face** — without writing complex code.

☐ Types of Enrichment You'll Perform

Enrichment Type	What It Does	Example
Cleaning	Fix typos, remove noise, standardize formatting	Turns "thnks! u rock!!" → "Thanks! You're awesome!"
Translation	Converts text from one language to another	French → English
Classification	Labels the content by topic, tone, or category	"Tutorial", "Complaint", "Review"

✅ Step-by-Step: Enrich with AI

Let's assume you've already extracted raw content like this:

```json
{
  "source_url": "https://example.com/article",
  "content": "bonjour! je cherche à automatiser mes emails."
}
```

☐ 1. Cleaning with OpenAI

Use OpenAI to rewrite text with proper formatting and grammar.

▶☐ Add OpenAI Node

- **Model**: gpt-3.5-turbo
- **System Prompt**:

  ```pgsql
  You are an editor. Clean the following text by fixing
  grammar, punctuation, and typos.
  ```

- **User Message**:

  ```bash
  ```

70

```
{{$json["content"]}}
```

✅ Output:

"Bonjour! Je cherche à automatiser mes emails."

⬚ 2. Translating with OpenAI or Hugging Face

Option A: OpenAI Translation

- **System Prompt**:

  ```css
  You are a translator. Translate the text from French to
  English.
  ```

- **User Message**:

  ```bash
  {{$json["content"]}}
  ```

✅ Output:

"Hello! I'm looking to automate my emails."

Option B: Hugging Face Translation Model

- Use model: `Helsinki-NLP/opus-mt-fr-en`
- Task: `translation`
- Input: `{{$json["content"]}}`

Same result — just using Hugging Face instead of OpenAI.

□□ 3. Classification with OpenAI

Let's categorize the content.

►□ Add OpenAI Node

- **System Prompt**:

  sql

  ```
  You are an AI that classifies text into one of these
  categories: Automation, Support, Feedback, Spam.
  Return only the category.
  ```

- **User Message**:

  bash

  ```
  {{$json["content"]}}
  ```

✅ Output:

"Automation"

□ Alternative: Use Hugging Face for Zero-Shot Classification

►□ Model:

```
facebook/bart-large-mnli
```

►□ Task:

```
zero-shot-classification
```

►□ Labels:

json

```
["Automation", "Support", "Feedback", "Spam"]
```

▶☐ Input:

```json
{{$json["content"]}}
```

✅ Hugging Face returns a ranked list of categories with confidence scores.

☐ Combine Enrichments (Optional)

Add multiple AI nodes in sequence:

```text
[Input: Raw Content]
     ↓
[OpenAI: Clean]
     ↓
[OpenAI: Translate]
     ↓
[OpenAI or HF: Classify]
     ↓
[Set: Combine All Enriched Fields]
```

Example output:

```json
{
  "cleaned_text": "Bonjour! Je cherche à automatiser mes emails.",
  "translation": "Hello! I'm looking to automate my emails.",
  "category": "Automation"
}
```

📌 Tips for High-Quality Enrichment

Tip	Why It Helps
Use clear, focused prompts	Reduces ambiguity in output
Limit AI outputs to one value	Helps with tagging/classification consistency

Tip	Why It Helps
Clean before classifying	Dirty text → noisy categories
Log raw + enriched content	Helps in debugging and future training

 Recap

You now know how to:

- Clean up raw text using OpenAI
- Translate content between languages
- Categorize or label content automatically
- Chain enrichments together before saving

Your data is now ready for structured storage — which we'll handle in **6.3**.

6.3 Sending Enriched Results to a Database or Spreadsheet

Goal: Take the output of your AI-enriched workflow (summarized, translated, or categorized data), and **store it automatically** into a system where it can be tracked, reviewed, or analyzed — like:

- Google Sheets (easy sharing)
- Airtable (collaboration + filtering)
- SQL DB (structured, scalable storage)

☐ Why Store Enriched Results?

Benefit	How It Helps
☐ Keep a record of enriched data	For reporting, auditing, or future training datasets
⚲ Enable search and filtering	Filter by sentiment, language, summary keywords
☐ Share with teams	Easily share via Airtable or Sheets

Benefit	How It Helps
⚙ Power downstream automations	Trigger follow-up emails, alerts, or workflows

✅ Step-by-Step: Store Enriched Output

Let's assume you have AI-enhanced data with fields like:

json

```
{
  "source_url": "https://example.com/post",
  "summary": "This article explains how to use n8n for
automation.",
  "language": "English",
  "category": "Tutorial"
}
```

Option 1: ■ Send to Google Sheets

▶ Step 1: Add Google Sheets Node

- Operation: `Append Row`
- Connect your Google account
- Select your spreadsheet + worksheet

▶ Step 2: Map fields

- A: `{{$json["source_url"]}}`
- B: `{{$json["summary"]}}`
- C: `{{$json["language"]}}`
- D: `{{$json["category"]}}`

✅ Every time the workflow runs, a new row is added to the sheet.

☐ Tip: Create column headers in row 1 beforehand.

Option 2: 📋 Send to Airtable

▶️☐ Step 1: Add Airtable Node

- Operation: `Create Record`
- Base: Select your Airtable base
- Table: e.g., `Enriched Articles`

▶️☐ Step 2: Map fields

- `Source: {{$json["source_url"]}}`
- `Summary: {{$json["summary"]}}`
- `Tags: {{$json["category"]}}`

✅ Airtable lets you filter and view records visually — great for team collaboration.

Option 3: 🗄️ Send to SQL Database

▶️☐ Step 1: Add PostgreSQL or MySQL Node

- Operation: `Insert`
- Table: e.g., `enriched_data`
- Ensure your DB schema has columns for each field

▶️☐ Step 2: Map fields

```json
{
  "source_url": "{{$json["source_url"]}}",
  "summary": "{{$json["summary"]}}",
  "language": "{{$json["language"]}}",
  "category": "{{$json["category"]}}"
}
```

✅ Great for scalable, production-grade storage.

☐ Optional Enhancements

Feature	Node / Idea
✅ De-duplicate entries	Use IF + check if URL or ID already exists
☐ Add timestamp	Use Set node with `new Date()`
☐ Export weekly reports	Trigger sheet export or Airtable view
🔔 Alert on specific tags	Notify if category = "Urgent"

☐ Sample Final Workflow:

```text
[HTTP Request / Sheet / Email Input]
        ↓
[AI: OpenAI or Hugging Face Enrichment]
        ↓
[Set / Function: Format Fields]
        ↓
[Store: Google Sheets / Airtable / DB]
```

✅ Recap

You now know how to:

- Push AI-enriched content to structured destinations
- Map and format data for Google Sheets, Airtable, or SQL
- Automate logging, analysis, and sharing of enriched results

This turns your AI pipeline into a full, production-ready **data intelligence system**.

Chapter 7: Project 4 – Chatbot with Memory

7.1 Building a Basic Chatbot with OpenAI

Goal: Build a basic chatbot that takes a user message, sends it to OpenAI, and returns a smart reply — all inside a single n8n workflow.

We'll use:

- `Webhook node` as the chat entry point
- `OpenAI node` to generate a response
- `Webhook Response node` to send back the reply

☐ What Makes It a "Chatbot"?

A chatbot:

1. Accepts user input
2. Understands context (even if minimal)
3. Generates a meaningful, relevant response
4. Optionally remembers previous interactions (memory)

In this section, we'll handle steps 1–3. Memory will come in Section 7.2.

☐☐ Step-by-Step: Build the Basic Chatbot

▶☐ Step 1: Add a Webhook Node

- **HTTP Method**: POST
- **Path**: /chatbot-basic
- This will allow users (or apps) to send chat messages to your n8n workflow.

Expected input:

json

```
{
  "message": "What is n8n used for?"
}
```

►□ Step 2: Add an OpenAI Node

- **Model**: gpt-3.5-turbo
- **System Prompt**:

  css

  ```
  You are a helpful chatbot assistant. Answer clearly and
  concisely.
  ```

- **User Message**:

  js

  ```
  {{$json["message"]}}
  ```

This sends the user's message to OpenAI and receives a smart reply.

►□ Step 3: Add a Webhook Response Node

This node sends OpenAI's reply back to the user.

- **Response Body**:

  js

  ```
  {
    "reply": {{$json["message"]}}
  }
  ```

✓ The user gets the chatbot's reply in the response body.

☐ Example Input & Output

POST to `https://your-n8n.com/webhook/chatbot-basic`
Request Body:

```json
{ "message": "What can I automate with n8n?" }
```

OpenAI Output:

"With n8n, you can automate tasks like email processing, API integrations, data syncing, and AI-powered workflows."

Webhook Response:

```json
{ "reply": "With n8n, you can automate tasks like..." }
```

📌 Add-On Features (Optional)

Feature	How To Add
✅ Typing delay	Use a `Delay` node before replying (simulates thinking)
☐ Personality tuning	Adjust the system prompt to change tone or behavior
🔒 Rate limiting	Add an "If" node to restrict messages per minute
📓 Message logging	Use a Google Sheets or Notion node to log chats

☐ Full Basic Chatbot Flow

```text
[Webhook: POST /chatbot-basic]
       ↓
[OpenAI: Generate reply]
       ↓
[Webhook Response: Send reply]
```

✅ Recap

You now have a working chatbot that:

- Accepts user input via webhook
- Sends it to OpenAI
- Returns a dynamic, context-aware response

This sets the stage for a more powerful chatbot with **memory**, coming up in the next section.

7.2 Adding Context/Memory Using n8n's Workflow Features

Goal: Turn your simple chatbot into a **conversational assistant** by storing and recalling previous messages within the same conversation thread.

This adds *memory* to your chatbot — so it can reply with context instead of treating each message like a new topic.

▢ How Memory Works in Chatbots

Memory Type	Description
Short-term	Remembers messages during one session or thread (e.g., a single chat)
Long-term	Stores info across sessions (e.g., user preferences, name, last question)

In this section, we'll implement **short-term memory** using n8n's built-in tools — no database or plugin needed.

🎁 Strategy: Store Context in a Variable or Storage Node

We'll:

1. Identify the user (via email, user ID, or IP)
2. Store the chat history (e.g., last 3 messages)
3. Inject that history into the OpenAI prompt
4. Return the AI's reply

🔲🔲 Step-by-Step: Add Chat Memory

▶🔲 Step 1: Accept a User ID in the Webhook

Update your Webhook node to expect something like:

json

```
{
  "user_id": "user_123",
  "message": "What's a workflow?"
}
```

▶🔲 Step 2: Add a Get Memory Step

Use a **n8n Data node** like:

- `Get Workflow Static Data` (temporary memory)
- or a simple `Read from Google Sheet` / `Read from Redis` (for persistent memory)

If using workflow memory:

js

```js
const staticData = $getWorkflowStaticData('global');
const userId = $json["user_id"];
return [{
  json: {
    history: staticData[userId] || []
  }
```

```
}];
```

▶☐ Step 3: Prepare a Prompt with History

Add a **Set Node** to construct a message for OpenAI like:

```js
const history = $json["history"];
const userMessage = $json["message"];

const prompt = [
  { role: "system", content: "You are a helpful assistant."
},
  ...history,
  { role: "user", content: userMessage }
];

return [{ json: { messages: prompt } }];
```

This feeds previous exchanges *plus* the current message into the OpenAI node.

▶☐ Step 4: Add OpenAI Node

- Use the `gpt-3.5-turbo` model
- Set **mode** to "Chat"
- **Messages**: `{{$json["messages"]}}`

✓ OpenAI now sees full context for this conversation.

▶☐ Step 5: Save New Message and Reply to Memory

Use a **Function Node** to update chat history:

```js
const staticData = $getWorkflowStaticData('global');
const userId = $json["user_id"];
```

```
const newMessage = {
  role: "user",
  content: $json["original_user_message"]
};
const reply = {
  role: "assistant",
  content: $json["openai_response"]
};

staticData[userId] = [...(staticData[userId] || []),
newMessage, reply].slice(-6); // keep last 6 turns

return [{ json: { reply: reply.content } }];
```

☐ Keeping only the last few messages helps avoid token limits in OpenAI.

▶☐ Step 6: Send Back the Reply

Use a **Webhook Response** node:

json

```
{
  "reply": "{{$json['reply']}}"
}
```

✅ Result: Chatbot with Memory!

The bot now:

- Knows the current user
- Remembers the past few exchanges
- Responds based on full conversation history

☐ Example Interaction

User:

"What's n8n?"

Bot:

"n8n is an automation tool that lets you connect apps and APIs visually."

User:

"Cool. Can I use it with OpenAI?"

✅ Bot remembers you just asked about n8n, and gives a relevant follow-up.

☐ Optional Enhancements

Feature	How to Do It
Long-term memory	Store chat history in Notion, Airtable, or DB
Human hand-off	Add condition to escalate to agent if AI fails
Memory expiration	Clear history after inactivity using a `Wait` node
Memory per session	Use session IDs if multiple users share a webhook

---

✅ Recap

You just:

- Built a working chatbot
- Gave it memory using n8n's static data + logic nodes
- Enabled real conversational flows powered by OpenAI

This is the core of intelligent assistants — no external DB required.

7.3 Logging Conversations to Notion or Airtable

Goal: Automatically log every user message and AI response into a structured system like **Notion** or **Airtable**, so you can:

- Review past conversations
- Track support history
- Analyze chatbot usage
- Personalize replies in future chats

▢ Why Log Conversations?

Benefit	What It Enables
📜 Audit trail	Review what the bot said and when
▢ Personalization	Greet returning users or reference prior questions
📊 Analytics	See which topics come up most often
💬 Human hand-off	Let agents view the full chat if escalation is needed

---

▢ What You'll Store

Each row in your table should include:

Field	Example
user_id	user_123
Timestamp	2025-03-24T14:03:00Z
user_input	"Can I use this bot for Slack?"
bot_reply	"Yes, n8n can connect to Slack using the Slack node."
session_id	session_abc123 *(optional)*

📋 Option 1: Logging to Airtable

▶▢ Step 1: Add Airtable Node

- Operation: `Create Record`
- Connect to your **Airtable base**
- Select the table (e.g., `Chat Logs`)

▶□ Step 2: Map Fields

```json
json

{
  "User ID": {{$json["user_id"]}},
  "Timestamp": {{$now}},
  "User Message": {{$json["original_user_message"]}},
  "Bot Reply": {{$json["reply"]}}
}
```

✓ Each conversation is stored as a new row.

□□ Option 2: Logging to Notion

▶□ Step 1: Add Notion Node

- Operation: `Create Page`
- Select your Notion database (e.g., `Chatbot Logs`)

▶□ Step 2: Map Properties

- **Title**: `Chat with {{$json["user_id"]}}`
- **Message**: `{{$json["original_user_message"]}}`
- **Response**: `{{$json["reply"]}}`
- **Time**: `{{$now}}`

✓ You now have a fully searchable, timestamped Notion record.

□ Optional: Append to Ongoing Thread

You can group messages by `session_id` or `user_id` and:

- Use `Update Record` (Airtable)
- Use `Update Page` or `Append Block` (Notion API)

This creates a rolling log of conversation history in one place.

☐ Quick Test: Log a Message

1. Add a **Set Node** with dummy user/chat data
2. Pass it through Airtable or Notion node
3. Confirm a row or page is created with the correct fields

✅ You're ready to automate real conversations.

☐ Bonus Ideas

Feature	How To Add
Tag by intent or topic	Add an OpenAI classification step
Flag messages for review	If reply contains keywords → log with "Needs Review"
Send daily summaries	Schedule n8n to extract and email reports
Add a feedback rating	Capture from user input → log alongside conversation

---

✅ Recap

You now have:

- A memory-enabled chatbot
- That logs every interaction
- Into Airtable or Notion for visibility and insights

This unlocks personalization, traceability, and better user support.

Chapter 8: Advanced AI Workflows

8.1 Chaining Multiple AI Tools (OpenAI + Hugging Face)

Goal: Build a workflow where different AI tools work together — for example:

- Use **Hugging Face** for classification or filtering
- Then pass the result to **OpenAI** for advanced generation or response
- Or vice versa, depending on the task

This lets you leverage **precision where needed** (Hugging Face) and **creativity where it shines** (OpenAI).

🔍 When Should You Chain AI Tools?

Use Case	Step 1	Step 2
Route based on topic	Hugging Face classification	OpenAI generates reply
Translate then summarize	Hugging Face translation	OpenAI summarizes
Filter toxic input before responding	Hugging Face toxicity check	OpenAI reply only if clean
Add structured tags, then generate content	Hugging Face tagging	OpenAI content generation

---

⬜⬜ Step-by-Step: Build a Chained AI Workflow

Use Case: Auto-reply only to positive customer feedback

▶⬜ Step 1: Trigger (Webhook or Gmail)

You receive a user message like:

```json
json

{
  "message": "Absolutely love the new feature! Great job."
}
```

▶☐ Step 2: Hugging Face Node – Sentiment Analysis

- **Model**: distilbert-base-uncased-finetuned-sst-2-english
- **Task**: text-classification
- **Input**: {{$json["message"]}}

Result:

```json
json

{
  "label": "POSITIVE",
  "score": 0.97
}
```

▶☐ Step 3: If Node – Only Continue if POSITIVE

Condition:

```js
js

{{$json["label"] === "POSITIVE"}}
```

✅ This filters input so only positive feedback moves forward.

▶☐ Step 4: OpenAI Node – Generate Reply

- **System Prompt**:

```sql
sql

You are a cheerful assistant. Thank the user for their
positive feedback and mention it helps the team.
```

- **User Message**:

```bash
{{$json["message"]}}
```

Output:

"Thanks so much for the kind words! We're thrilled to hear you're enjoying the new feature — feedback like this keeps us going!"

▶□ Step 5: Send Email or Webhook Response

You can now send the generated reply via:

- Email node
- Webhook response
- Slack message

□ Alternate Example: Translate → Classify → Reply

```text
[Input: French Message]
    ↓
[Hugging Face: Translate fr → en]
    ↓
[Hugging Face: Classify Topic]
    ↓
[OpenAI: Generate Reply]
```

💡 Great for international feedback or multilingual surveys.

☐ Pro Tips

Tip	Why It Helps
Keep AI tools focused	Hugging Face for labels, OpenAI for generation
Use `Set` nodes to format data	Helps standardize input between tools
Add `If` nodes to control flow	Avoid wasting tokens when conditions aren't met
Log both raw + enriched data	Great for audits, feedback, and training

☐ Challenge: Build Your Own Chained AI Workflow

Try this:

- Input: Product review from a webhook
- Hugging Face: Detect sentiment
- If negative: Use OpenAI to draft an apology email
- If positive: Use OpenAI to generate a thank-you message
- Store reply + sentiment in Google Sheets

✅ Recap

In this section, you learned how to:

- Chain multiple AI tools inside one n8n workflow
- Combine the accuracy of Hugging Face with the creativity of OpenAI
- Control flow with conditions to optimize API usage and logic

This approach gives you **fine-grained AI automation with flexibility**.

8.2 Using Code Nodes for Custom Logic

Goal: Learn how to use **JavaScript-powered Code Nodes** in n8n to:

- Preprocess data before passing to AI
- Post-process OpenAI or Hugging Face responses
- Create dynamic control flow
- Add validation, formatting, or filtering logic

□ Code Node Types in n8n

Node	Purpose	Runs On
Function Node	Manipulates an array of items	All items together
FunctionItem	Modifies each item individually	One at a time

Use `Function` for logic that compares multiple items.
Use `FunctionItem` for per-message processing (which is common in AI workflows).

□□ Example Use Cases for Code Nodes

Use Case	Example Code Node Task
□ Clean messy text before prompt	Strip HTML, emojis, long whitespace
𝗜𝗶𝗹 Validate AI classification	Discard or reroute low-confidence responses
□ Build custom memory prompts	Concatenate conversation history into chat format
□ Control flow dynamically	Route items based on score, confidence, or keywords

93

▶□ Step-by-Step: Clean AI Output with a Function Node

Let's say OpenAI replies with some extra newlines or fluff you want to clean before sending the reply.

OpenAI Output:

```json
json

{
  "message": "\n\nSure! Here's what I found:\n\nThe tool
you're asking about is..."
}
```

Add a Function Node:

```javascript
javascript

return items.map(item => {
  const raw = item.json.message || '';
  const cleaned = raw
    .trim()
    .replace(/\n{2,}/g, '\n\n')  // Normalize line breaks
    .replace(/^Sure! Here's what I found:\s*/i, ''); //
Remove boilerplate

  item.json.cleaned_message = cleaned;
  return item;
});
```

Use in Email or Webhook:

```js
js

{{$json["cleaned_message"]}}
```

✅ Cleaner, more human-friendly replies!

☐ Example 2: Custom AI Classification Validator

After using Hugging Face or OpenAI for classification:

```json
json

{
  "category": "Feedback",
  "confidence": 0.54
}
```

You want to skip or flag if confidence < 0.7.

Add a FunctionItem Node:

```javascript
javascript

const confidence = item.json.confidence || 0;

if (confidence < 0.7) {
  // Add a flag for manual review
  item.json.flagged = true;
} else {
  item.json.flagged = false;
}

return item;
```

Then add an **If Node**:

- `flagged == false` → Proceed to auto-routing
- `flagged == true` → Log or alert a human

☐ Example 3: Construct Multi-Message Chat Memory

Want to format message history for OpenAI like a proper chat?

95

Use a Function Node:

```javascript
javascript

const history = [
  { role: 'user', content: 'What is n8n?' },
  { role: 'assistant', content: 'It's a workflow automation
tool.' },
  { role: 'user', content: 'Can I use it with AI?' }
];

const currentMessage = $json["message"];

return [{
  json: {
    messages: [
      ...history,
      { role: 'user', content: currentMessage }
    ]
  }
}];
```

Send `{{$json["messages"]}}` to OpenAI in **Chat Mode**.

📌 Tips for Using Code Nodes Safely

Tip	Why It Helps
Use `FunctionItem` for simplicity	One input → one output
Always `return` an array	Even for single items
Test with real data	Catch edge cases and null values
Use `console.log()` for debugging	Logs appear in the execution details
Keep it readable	Add comments for team understanding

✅ Recap

With Code Nodes, you can:

- Add custom logic to clean, transform, or route data
- Enhance AI output before presentation

- Combine memory, filters, or formatting logic easily

Function Nodes are your "JavaScript toolbox" inside n8n.

8.3 Handling Rate Limits and Errors

Goal: Make your AI-powered automations in n8n more stable and production-ready by:

- Catching errors
- Retrying failed calls
- Handling rate limits
- Logging or alerting on critical issues

□ Common AI API Failures

Error Type	What It Means	Examples
Rate Limit (429)	Too many requests in a short time	OpenAI's free tier, Hugging Face API
Timeout (504)	Server didn't respond in time	Large prompt or high model load
Invalid Input (400)	Bad formatting or missing prompt	Empty message, malformed JSON
Auth Error (401/403)	Invalid or expired token	Bad API key, revoked access

✅ Strategy: Handle Failures the n8n Way

n8n gives you tools to **catch and manage errors** in your workflow logic, such as:

Tool / Feature	What It Does
Error Workflow	A separate workflow triggered when a node fails
Try-Catch Structure	Manual error branches using `Error` trigger
Retry Settings	Retry failed API calls automatically (per node)

Tool / Feature	What It Does
If Nodes	Check responses and route logic conditionally
Webhook Alerts	Notify you via Slack, Email, or SMS if things break

□ Step-by-Step: Add Retry + Fallback Logic

▶□ Step 1: Enable Retry on OpenAI or Hugging Face Node

Click on the **OpenAI Node → Settings tab**
Under **Retry on Fail**, set:

- **Max Attempts**: 3
- **Interval Between Attempts**: 2000 ms (2 seconds)

✅ This helps handle **temporary rate limits** or random outages.

▶□ Step 2: Catch Errors with an Error Workflow

1. Create a new workflow
2. Add a **"Error Trigger" node**
3. Add actions like:
   - Send Email: "OpenAI node failed"
   - Log error in Notion/Sheets
   - Retry logic or human alert

In your main workflow, go to **Settings → On Error**, and choose your error-handling workflow.

▶□ Step 3: Use an "If" Node to Handle Bad AI Output

Sometimes OpenAI or Hugging Face returns gibberish or empty values.

Add an **If Node** after your AI node:

```js
js
```

```
{{$json["message"] !== ""}}
```

- **If true** → Continue workflow
- **If false** → Fallback message or retry with a simpler prompt

---

▶□ Step 4: Add a Delay to Manage Rate Limits

If you're sending **multiple AI requests** in a loop:

Add a **Delay Node** (e.g., 1–2 seconds) between calls to avoid hitting rate limits.

▶□ Step 5: Notify on Persistent Errors

Add a **Slack, Email, or SMS node** if:

- A node fails
- A specific condition is not met (e.g., missing response)
- Retries fail and user needs to be alerted

Example Slack message:

```php
php
```

```
AI Workflow Failed
User: {{$json["user_id"]}}
Reason: No response from OpenAI
```

□ Bonus: Build a Smart Retry Flow with a Fallback Prompt

Add an **If Node** to check if OpenAI's reply is missing.

If missing:

- Route to a **secondary OpenAI node** with a simpler or backup prompt:

```sql
You are a fallback assistant. If the previous prompt
failed, reply briefly with: "We're reviewing your
request and will follow up soon."
```

✅ Keeps your chatbot responsive even under failure conditions.

📌 Best Practices for AI Workflow Resilience

Practice	Why It Matters
Use retry settings per node	Avoid manual loops for recoverable errors
Log failures + inputs	Helps you debug why the AI failed
Catch empty/malformed responses	Prevents downstream nodes from crashing
Delay between AI calls	Reduces chance of hitting rate limits
Always have a fallback path	Ensures user gets *something* back

---

✅ Recap

You now know how to:

- Use built-in retries for API stability
- Create custom error workflows in n8n
- Check and respond to bad or empty AI outputs
- Notify yourself when something breaks

This gives your AI workflows **the reliability they need for real-world use**.

Chapter 9: Deploying and Monitoring Workflows

9.1 Running on Cloud or Server

Goal: Learn how to run your n8n instance continuously on the cloud or your own server so your workflows (especially AI-powered ones) stay live and responsive — 24/7.

☁️ Deployment Options for n8n

Deployment Type	Description	Best For
n8n Cloud (official)	Fully managed SaaS by the n8n team	Easiest setup, low-maintenance
Self-hosted (Docker)	Run n8n on any server or VPS using Docker	More control, lower cost
n8n Desktop App	Local testing with GUI	Local development only
Cloud platforms	e.g., Render, Railway, Fly.io, AWS, etc.	Devs comfortable with cloud infra

---

✅ Option 1: Deploy on n8n Cloud

The easiest way to go live — hosted by the creators of n8n.

▶️ Steps:

1. Go to https://cloud.n8n.io
2. Sign up and create a workspace
3. Set your webhook paths (e.g., `/chatbot-basic`)
4. Add your credentials securely via the cloud dashboard
5. Enable **Production Mode** for always-on workflows

✅ Perfect for production use with zero DevOps.

🐳 Option 2: Deploy with Docker (Self-Hosted)

Run n8n on your own Linux server (e.g., DigitalOcean, Linode, EC2).

▶□ Prerequisites:

- Docker + Docker Compose installed
- Domain name (optional but recommended)
- Basic server access via SSH

▶□ Sample `docker-compose.yml`:

```yaml
yaml

version: '3.1'

services:
  n8n:
    image: n8nio/n8n
    restart: always
    ports:
      - "5678:5678"
    environment:
      - N8N_BASIC_AUTH_USER=admin
      - N8N_BASIC_AUTH_PASSWORD=securepassword
      - N8N_HOST=n8n.yourdomain.com
      - N8N_PORT=5678
      - WEBHOOK_URL=https://n8n.yourdomain.com/
    volumes:
      - ./n8n_data:/home/node/.n8n
```

Then run:

```bash
bash

docker-compose up -d
```

✅ n8n will be running at `http://your-server-ip:5678`
🔐 Secure with SSL using Nginx + Let's Encrypt (recommended).

☁️ Option 3: Use a Cloud Platform

You can deploy n8n using third-party platforms like:

Platform	Notes
Render	Simple Docker deployment, free tier available
Railway	Git-based deploys, great for quick testing
Fly.io	Scalable, edge-deployed apps with autoscaling
Heroku	Not officially supported, possible via Docker
AWS ECS	Advanced setup with full control

Each offers scalable deployment options with variable pricing.

🔐 Securing Your Workflow

Task	How to Do It
Basic auth	Set `N8N_BASIC_AUTH_USER`/`PASSWORD`
HTTPS	Use a reverse proxy (e.g., Nginx + SSL)
IP allow-listing	Use firewall or cloud access controls
Secrets & credentials	Store using n8n's encrypted vault

☐ Test Your Deployment

After deployment:

1. Open your deployed URL
2. Trigger a webhook (e.g., chatbot)
3. Verify OpenAI/Hugging Face calls still work
4. Check logs for any errors (`docker logs n8n` or platform logs)

☐ Pro Tips for Deployment

Tip	Why It Helps
Use `.env` file	Keep environment variables organized
Enable backups	Protect workflows and credentials
Keep workflows modular	Easier to debug and scale
Use subdomains for each instance	Clean and organized routing (e.g., `ai.n8n.com`)

✅ Recap

You now know how to:

- Run n8n reliably in the cloud or on your own server
- Choose between official cloud, Docker, or third-party platforms
- Secure and test your deployment for production use

9.2 Error Handling & Retries

This section ensures that your **production-grade AI workflows** in n8n can detect issues, retry failed operations, and **fail gracefully** without crashing the entire process.

9.2 Error Handling & Retries

Goal: Build resilient workflows by:

- Automatically retrying failed steps
- Logging or alerting when something goes wrong
- Preventing entire workflows from failing due to one bad node

☐ Why This Matters

AI APIs (like OpenAI or Hugging Face) can:

- Timeout
- Hit rate limits
- Return invalid responses
- Be unavailable temporarily

Without proper error handling, your automation could break silently or halt the entire workflow.

☐ Retry Built-In: Node Settings

Almost every node in n8n supports **automatic retry logic**.

▶☐ How to Enable Retries:

1. Click on a node (e.g., OpenAI or HTTP Request)
2. Go to the **"Settings" tab**
3. Under **Retry on Fail**, set:
   - **Max Attempts**: 3
   - **Wait Between Retries**: 2000 ms (2 seconds)

✅ This handles *temporary issues* like rate limits or network errors.

☐ Catching Failures with an Error Workflow

n8n lets you create a **global fallback workflow** to catch and handle failed runs.

▶☐ Steps:

1. Create a new workflow
2. Add an **"Error Trigger"** node

3. Add nodes to:
   - o Log the error to Google Sheets or Notion
   - o Send a Slack or Email alert
   - o Optionally retry or notify a human
4. Go back to your main workflow → click **Settings** → **Error Workflow** → select your new error handler.

☐ Manual Try/Catch Logic in a Single Workflow

Use `IF` nodes and branches to create **local error logic**.

Example:

- If OpenAI output is empty or invalid → use a fallback message.

```
text

[OpenAI Node]
    ↓
[If Node: reply exists?]
   ↙            ↘
[Send Reply]    [Use Default Reply + Log Error]
```

IF Condition:

```
js

{{$json["message"] !== ""}}
```

This keeps your chatbot or content workflow alive even when AI fails.

⊞ Log & Inspect Failed Inputs

Want to debug later? Log what caused the failure.

Add a Set Node:

```
json
```

```
{
  "error_type": "Empty AI reply",
  "user_input": {{$json["message"]}},
  "timestamp": {{$now}}
}
```

Then store it in:

- Google Sheets
- Airtable
- Notion
- A database (PostgreSQL, MySQL, Supabase, etc.)

💡 Optional: Exponential Backoff (for API Limits)

You can simulate **exponential backoff** using multiple Delay nodes:

```text
[Try 1 → Delay 1s → Try 2 → Delay 4s → Try 3 → Delay 8s]
```

Or use a custom Function node to dynamically set retry delays.

☐ Best Practices for Error-Resilient AI Workflows

Practice	Why It Helps
Always enable retry on API nodes	Prevents temporary failures from halting flow
Use fallback messages	Keeps user experience smooth
Log failed input/output	Helps diagnose issues
Alert your team on failure	Stay informed and proactive
Use error workflows	Centralizes failure handling

✅ Recap

You now know how to:

- Enable automatic retries per node
- Handle AI or logic errors gracefully
- Log and route errors to external systems
- Set up a global error-handling workflow

With these in place, your n8n AI workflows are **resilient, auditable, and production-ready**.

9.3 Workflow Logging and Versioning

Goal: Learn how to:

- Log inputs, outputs, and system actions for traceability
- Maintain versions of your workflows for safe updates and rollbacks
- Create an audit trail for your AI-powered automations

☐ Part 1: Logging Workflow Activity

Logging gives you **visibility** into how your workflow is performing and helps you:

- Troubleshoot failures
- Track AI outputs over time
- Audit user inputs
- Monitor behavior for compliance

▶□ What to Log

What to Log	Example
✦ User inputs	`"message": "How does n8n work?"`
✦ AI outputs	`"reply": "n8n is a workflow automation tool..."`
✦ Errors/fallbacks	`"error": "OpenAI returned empty message"`
✦ Timestamps	`"run_at": "2025-03-24T10:42:15Z"`
✦ Execution details	Node status, run duration, webhook paths

▶□ Where to Log

Destination	Best For
Google Sheets	Easy viewing, lightweight logs
Airtable	Filtering and tagging logs
Notion	Full chat-like context history
SQL DB / Supabase	Advanced querying and scaling
File / S3	Archiving historical logs

▶□ Example: Log to Google Sheets

1. Add a **Set Node**:

```json
json

{
  "user_input": {{$json["user_input"]}},
  "ai_reply": {{$json["reply"]}},
  "timestamp": {{$now}}
}
```

2. Add a **Google Sheets Node**:

- Operation: `Append Row`
- Map the fields to columns

✅ Your workflow now has a complete record of every interaction.

🌀 Part 2: Workflow Versioning in n8n

n8n tracks changes to workflows automatically, and you can also export versions manually for Git-based control.

▶️ Built-In Workflow History

1. Go to your workflow in n8n
2. Click **"Versions"** in the top bar
3. You'll see:
   - A full history of changes
   - Who made each change
   - The ability to restore previous versions

✅ Use this to roll back a bad edit or compare versions over time.

▶️ Manual Versioning (Advanced)

You can also export your workflow and manage versions in a Git repo.

1. Click the three-dot menu → **"Download workflow"**
2. Save it as `workflow-v1.json`, `workflow-v2.json`, etc.
3. Commit to Git with comments:

```sql
git commit -m "Add retry logic to OpenAI node"
```

✅ Great for teams, audits, or collaboration across environments.

☐ Pro Tips for Workflow Logging & Versioning

Tip	Why It Helps
Add log entries after every AI node	See what the model actually responded
Track run duration with timestamps	Helps detect performance issues
Annotate version changes clearly	Useful when debugging why logic was modified
Use consistent log formats	Easier to parse and analyze later
Backup key workflows weekly	Protects against accidental overwrites

✅ Recap

You now know how to:

- Log every step of your workflow for traceability and audit
- Use n8n's built-in versioning for safe workflow updates
- Export and version-control workflows using Git
- Choose smart destinations (Notion, Sheets, DB) for your logs

This makes your n8n AI system **observable, reliable, and maintainable** over the long term.

Chapter 10: Best Practices and Tips

10.1 Designing AI Workflows Responsibly

AI automation is powerful — but with great power comes great responsibility. This section focuses on **how to build AI workflows in n8n that are ethical, reliable, and safe** for both users and your business.

☐ Why Responsible Design Matters

Risk	What Can Happen
💬 Inaccurate AI replies	Mislead users or damage trust
☐⚖☐ Biased classifications	Unfair decisions, reputational risk
☐ Infinite loops or spam	Blow up APIs or inboxes
☐ Lack of transparency	No traceability or audit trail
🔒 Exposure of sensitive info	Leaks from AI prompts or misconfigured logs

Responsible AI workflow design ensures you **build automation that's accurate, fair, secure, and traceable.**

✅ Principles for Responsible AI Workflow Design

---

1. Human-in-the-Loop Where Needed

Don't trust AI blindly — give humans the final say for:

- Critical decisions (e.g., rejecting users, issuing refunds)
- Low-confidence predictions
- Sensitive content generation

☐☐ Add **approval steps** using If nodes + Email/Slack alerts.

---

2. Validate AI Outputs Before Acting on Them

AI can "hallucinate" or return bad results.

Use:

- **If nodes** to check for empty, vague, or irrelevant outputs
- **Regex or keyword checks** to validate format
- **Fallbacks** like "Sorry, I didn't get that. Can you rephrase?"

☐ Example: After OpenAI response → If message doesn't include keywords like "Thanks" → use default reply.

---

3. Log Everything (Inputs + Outputs)

For audit, transparency, and debugging.

Log:

- The original user input
- AI-generated outputs
- Timestamp + version of the workflow
- Any overrides or fallback usage

☐ Store in Google Sheets, Notion, or a secure DB.

---

4. Respect User Data and Privacy

Avoid sending sensitive data to AI models, especially 3rd-party APIs like OpenAI.

- Mask PII (e.g., emails, phone numbers) before sending to the AI node
- Use environment variables to store keys securely

- Add disclaimer if content is AI-generated

🔐 Bonus: Add a "scrub data" step before AI nodes using a FunctionItem node.

---

5. Use Clear Prompts with Constraints

To prevent unpredictable output:

- Keep prompts short and focused
- Use strict instructions ("Reply in one sentence")
- Set expectations ("If unsure, say 'I'm not sure'")

☐ Example:

css

```
You are a helpful assistant. Answer in a polite, professional
tone. Never speculate if information is missing.
```

---

6. Implement Rate Limits and Quotas

Prevent abuse or accidental loops:

- Use **IF + Counter** logic to block after X uses
- Add **Delay nodes** to pace API calls
- Track usage per user with IDs or IPs

☐ Tip: For public bots, add daily/session usage limits per user.

---

7. Explain When AI is Used

Be transparent with users:

- Add a note: "This response was generated by an AI assistant"
- Especially for public-facing emails, chats, or summaries

☐☐ Builds trust and sets expectations

📌 Checklist: Responsible AI Workflow Design

✅ Use fallback responses
✅ Log inputs and outputs
✅ Add human approval steps when needed
✅ Limit prompt length and scope
✅ Mask or exclude sensitive info
✅ Validate AI output before acting
✅ Monitor API usage + error rates
✅ Keep your models and prompts updated

✅ Recap

In this section, you learned how to:

- Think through the risks of AI automation
- Add safeguards like validation, logging, and fallbacks
- Design flows that are secure, auditable, and fair

Building **responsible AI workflows** isn't just ethical — it makes your systems more **reliable**, **trustworthy**, and **scalable**.

10.2 API Key Safety

When using AI services like OpenAI, Hugging Face, or any external platform in n8n, your **API keys** are the keys to the kingdom. If exposed or misused, they can lead to:

- Unauthorized usage (skyrocketing bills 💸)
- Data leaks
- Service lockouts
- Reputational damage

This section walks you through **best practices to securely manage API keys** in your n8n AI workflows.

🔐 Why API Key Safety Matters

Risk	What Happens
🔒 Key exposed in workflows	Anyone can use your API, potentially maxing out quotas
☐ Hard-coded in Function node	Key is visible to other users/devs in n8n
☐ Shared in public links	Workflow exports or public docs leak the key
☐ Misuse via webhooks	Keys tied to open webhooks can be abused

---

✅ Best Practices for API Key Safety in n8n

---

1. Use Built-In Credential Management

n8n has secure credential storage for services like:

- OpenAI
- Hugging Face
- Google Sheets
- HTTP Auth / API Key

▶☐ Steps:

- Go to **Credentials → New Credential**
- Select the integration (e.g., OpenAI API)
- Enter your API key (it's stored encrypted)
- Link it to the appropriate node(s)

✓ This keeps the key **out of the workflow code**.

---

2. Never Hard-Code API Keys in Function or Set Nodes

⊘ **Avoid this:**

```javascript
const apiKey = "sk-abc123-xyz456"; // ✗ BAD
```

If someone accesses your workflow, they can **see and copy** the key.

✓ Instead, use environment variables or stored credentials.

---

3. Use `.env` Files for Self-Hosted Instances

If running n8n via Docker or on your own server:

- Store keys in a `.env` file:

```env
OPENAI_API_KEY=sk-abc123-xyz456
```

- Reference it in the workflow using `process.env.OPENAI_API_KEY` *(or create a global environment variable and use it via a Function node)*

✓ Keeps sensitive data **out of code and UI**.

---

4. Restrict API Keys at the Source

On platforms like OpenAI or Hugging Face, **limit what your key can do**:

Platform	API Key Restrictions to Set
OpenAI	Limit to certain endpoints or usage caps
Hugging Face	Use read-only or sandboxed keys if possible
Google APIs	Restrict by IP, domain, or service scope

✅ Reduces damage even if a key is leaked.

---

5. Rotate and Revoke Keys Regularly

Task	How Often
☐ Rotate keys	Every 30–90 days
☐ Remove unused	Monthly
🚫 Revoke on exposure	Immediately

✅ Keep your system safe even if someone accidentally leaks a key.

---

6. Don't Include Keys in Workflow Exports

When exporting workflows:

- **Uncheck "Include credentials"** unless strictly necessary
- Never share keys in shared `.json` files or public GitHub repos

✅ Prevents accidental leaks during collaboration or publishing.

---

7. Monitor API Usage and Set Limits

Use your API provider's dashboard to:

- Monitor recent activity
- Set **usage limits**
- Enable **notifications** for unusual patterns

✅ Helps catch misuse before it becomes expensive.

🔍 Bonus: Obscure Webhook URLs

If a webhook triggers an AI call tied to your API key:

- Make the URL **unpredictable** (e.g., `/webhook/ai-bot-93x29ab`)
- Use **Basic Auth** or **Header Token Checks** for protection

```text
If Header: x-api-token != YOUR_SECRET → Block request
```

✅ Prevents public abuse of webhook-triggered AI calls.

✅ Recap

To protect your AI keys in n8n:

- Use **n8n's credential manager** — not Set/Function nodes
- Store sensitive keys in `.env` or secure vaults
- Restrict and rotate API keys regularly
- Never include keys in exports or share public workflow links with credentials
- Add usage limits and monitor activity in provider dashboards

With these steps, your n8n + AI setup will stay **secure, scalable, and production-ready**.

10.3 When Not to Use AI

Not every problem needs an AI solution. In fact, **adding AI where it isn't necessary** can increase costs, reduce reliability, and complicate workflows that could be solved with simple logic or built-in tools.

This section helps you recognize **when AI is overkill** — and when traditional automation gets the job done faster, cheaper, and more reliably.

⚠️ Why This Matters

Problem	Impact
☠ Overusing AI for simple tasks	Higher API costs, slower execution
🐢 Latency	AI responses take seconds, not milliseconds
✗ Unpredictable output	You can't always control what AI will say
☐ Complex for no reason	Adds unnecessary moving parts to your automation

Knowing **when not to use AI** is just as important as knowing when to use it.

✗ Don't Use AI For...

1. Simple Decision-Making or Routing

If you're routing based on clear rules like:

- "If email subject contains 'invoice', route to Finance"
- "If score is greater than 70%, approve"

✓ Use an **If node** or **Switch node** instead of AI.

2. Fixed Responses or Templates

If the response is always the same:

- "Thanks for your message, we'll get back to you."
- "Please restart the app and try again."

✓ Use a **Set node** or **pre-written response** — AI isn't needed.

---

3. Math or Structured Calculations

LLMs (like GPT) are **bad at math** and logic-heavy tasks like:

- Precise formulas
- Invoice total calculations
- Complex sorting or filtering

✓ Use **code nodes** or **spreadsheet logic** — it's faster and more accurate.

---

4. Validations That Require Precision

Example:

- "Is this a valid email address?"
- "Does this CSV match the expected format?"

✓ Use **regex**, built-in parsers, or **API validators** — more consistent than an LLM guess.

---

5. Heavily Regulated or High-Risk Actions

Avoid using AI for:

- Legal notices
- Medical advice
- Financial decisions
- Policy enforcement

✓ Always add a **human-in-the-loop** for high-stakes scenarios.

6. Tasks That Require Speed

Need instant responses (under 1 second)?

- Button clicks
- App-to-app sync
- Webhook pings

✓ AI may introduce delay — **use plain logic or caching** instead.

☐ Ask These Questions Before Using AI:

Question	Why Ask It?
Can a simple If/Set node solve this?	Avoid unnecessary complexity
Does it need creativity or flexibility?	AI shines here — if not, skip it
Is the result deterministic?	If yes, AI is likely not required
Will the output need to be audited?	Simple code is easier to trace
Do I care about latency/cost?	AI is slower and more expensive

✓ When AI *Is* Worth It

Use AI when:

- You need **natural language understanding**
- The task involves **summarizing, generating, or rephrasing**
- You want to **add flexibility** to user inputs or support forms
- The problem is **too fuzzy for rules** (e.g., "What's the tone of this message?")

☐ Example: Use Logic Instead of AI

Bad (Overkill):
Using OpenAI to classify:

"If email includes the word 'refund', route to Billing."

Better:
Use an `If Node`:

js

```
{{$json["email"].toLowerCase().includes("refund")}}
```

✅ Saves time, cost, and avoids hallucination.

✅ Recap

Don't use AI when:

- Rules are simple
- Outputs are fixed
- Speed or accuracy is critical
- The problem has no ambiguity
- There's a lower-cost, more stable alternative

Use AI when:

- The task is ambiguous, creative, or language-based
- You need flexible, human-like understanding
- Simpler logic would require tons of conditions

A well-designed AI workflow uses AI only where it adds real value.

Chapter 11: Exercises & Projects

11.1 Challenge Workflows (With Problem Description)

This section is all about **hands-on learning**. You'll get challenge prompts — real-world scenarios that force you to apply what you've learned throughout the book. Each problem includes a short description of the goal, the tools you can use, and tips (without giving away the full solution).

Perfect for practice, portfolio building, or team interviews.

☐ Challenge 1: AI-Powered Lead Qualifier Bot

📇 Scenario

You're receiving leads via a form (or email). Some are legit; others are spam, vague, or incomplete. You need to automatically **score the quality of each lead** and flag high-quality leads for follow-up.

⊛ Your Goal

- Classify each lead message into: `Qualified`, `Needs Review`, or `Spam`
- Send qualified leads to Google Sheets
- Notify your team via Slack for high-potential leads

☐ Tools You Should Use

- Webhook (or Gmail IMAP)
- Hugging Face (for classification or spam detection)
- OpenAI (to summarize message and decide if it's valuable)
- If node + Slack node

☐ Challenge 2: Multilingual Feedback Responder

Scenario

You're receiving customer feedback in multiple languages. You need to:

1. Translate it to English
2. Classify it (e.g., Praise, Complaint, Bug Report)
3. Send a **thank-you email** back in the **user's original language**

Your Goal

- Detect input language
- Use Hugging Face or OpenAI to translate and classify
- Use OpenAI to write a polite, short reply in the original language
- Send via Email node

Tools

- Hugging Face translation or OpenAI
- Google Sheets or CSV for input
- Language detection via OpenAI or custom logic
- Delay + Email nodes

Challenge 3: Content Enricher for Blog SEO

Scenario

You run a content team and want to enrich blog drafts by:

- Generating SEO tags
- Writing a 1-sentence summary
- Extracting 3 bullet points
- Suggesting a better title

All from a raw blog draft pulled from Notion or Google Docs.

Your Goal

- Input: Blog post content
- Output: tags, summary, bullets, improved title
- Store enriched version in Airtable or Notion

▢ Tools

- OpenAI (content enrichment)
- Notion or Google Docs input
- Airtable or Sheets output
- Set + Function nodes for formatting

▢ Challenge 4: Support Ticket Prioritizer + Summarizer

☝ Scenario

You receive dozens of support tickets daily. You need to:

- Prioritize tickets by urgency
- Generate a summary
- Route critical ones to Slack or Email

☉ Your Goal

- Input: Ticket message (via Sheet or API)
- Output: `Priority`, `Summary`, `Owner`
- Notify only if priority = High or customer is VIP

▢ Tools

- Hugging Face for classification
- OpenAI for summarization
- Sheets or DB for input
- Slack node for escalation

☐ Challenge 5: AI Daily Digest Generator

☛ Scenario

You pull articles from various RSS feeds. You want to:

- Summarize the top 5 daily articles
- Format into a clean digest email
- Send to a mailing list every morning at 8 AM

☞ Your Goal

- Fetch RSS feeds
- Use OpenAI to summarize each article
- Combine summaries into an email
- Automate with a Cron trigger (8 AM daily)

☐ Tools

- RSS node + Cron trigger
- OpenAI + Function node for formatting
- Email node for final output

💡 Tips for Working on These Challenges

Tip	Why It Helps
Start simple, then layer AI	Get the flow working with basic logic first
Use mock data	Don't wait for real inputs to test your flow
Log everything during testing	Helps you debug classification/summarization issues
Add delays between AI calls	Prevent rate limits or token errors
Think like a user	Test with realistic, messy input

✅ Recap

These challenges help you:

- Practice real-world automation
- Reinforce AI + logic skills from previous chapters
- Build portfolio-ready projects
- Create deployable tools for support, content, and productivity

11.2 Solutions walkthrough

Challenge 1: AI-Powered Lead Qualifier Bot

🔧 Step-by-Step Solution:

1. **Trigger**: Webhook node or IMAP Email node (captures new lead)
2. **Extract Fields**: Use a Set node to isolate `name`, `email`, `message`
3. **Classify Message**:
   - Hugging Face (zero-shot) or OpenAI:

     ```kotlin
     Classify this lead message as either: Qualified,
     Needs Review, or Spam.
     ```

4. **Add If Node**:
   - If `classification == "Qualified"` → go to Sheet + Slack
   - If `Spam` → end flow or log
5. **Summarize**: Use OpenAI to write a one-line summary
6. **Store in Google Sheet**: Append lead info + summary
7. **Slack Notification** (only if Qualified or high-value):

   ```bash
   New Qualified Lead:
   {{$json["name"]}} - {{$json["summary"]}}
   ```

✅ **Done:** You've automated lead filtering + routing using AI.

✅ Challenge 2: Multilingual Feedback Responder

🔧 Step-by-Step Solution:

1. **Trigger**: Webhook or Google Sheet with `message, language, email`
2. **Detect Language**:
   - Use OpenAI:

   ```kotlin
   What language is this message written in?
   ```

   - Or extract from form (if available)
3. **Translate to English**:
   - Hugging Face model (`fr-en`, `es-en`, etc.)
4. **Classify Feedback**:
   - OpenAI or Hugging Face zero-shot:
     - Categories: Praise, Complaint, Bug Report
5. **Generate Reply**:
   - Prompt OpenAI:

   ```pgsql
   Write a polite thank-you message in [original
   language] based on this message: "[translated
   feedback]"
   ```

6. **Send Email**: Use the Email node, map to `email` field

✅ **Done:** You've created a global, multilingual feedback handler.

✅ Challenge 3: Content Enricher for Blog SEO

🔧 Step-by-Step Solution:

1. **Trigger**: Pull content from Notion or Google Docs
2. **Clean Input**: Use Set or Function to extract raw text
3. **Enrich** with OpenAI:
   o Prompt:

```diff
For the following blog draft:
- Suggest 5 SEO tags
- Write a 1-sentence summary
- List 3 key bullet points
- Suggest an improved title
```

4. **Parse Output**: Use Function node or direct JSON formatting
5. **Store in Airtable**:
   o Columns: `Title, Summary, Tags, Bullets, Source URL`

✅ **Done:** You've automated blog post enhancement with AI.

✅ Challenge 4: Support Ticket Prioritizer + Summarizer

🔧 Step-by-Step Solution:

1. **Trigger**: Read tickets from Google Sheets or IMAP inbox
2. **Extract Content**: Use Set node for `message, customer_id`
3. **Classify Priority**:
   o Hugging Face or OpenAI prompt:

```kotlin
Classify this support ticket as: High, Medium,
Low priority.
```

4. **Summarize**:
   o Prompt OpenAI: "Summarize the issue in 1–2 lines."
5. **If Node**: If Priority == High or Customer == VIP → go to Slack
6. **Slack Message**:

```php
```

📷 High-Priority Ticket:
{{$json["summary"]}} - from {{$json["customer_id"]}}

7. **Store Full Output**: Append to Google Sheet or Notion for logs

✅ **Done:** You've built a smart ticket triager + alert system.

✅ Challenge 5: AI Daily Digest Generator

🔧 Step-by-Step Solution:

1. **Trigger**: Cron node → 8:00 AM daily
2. **Fetch Content**: RSS Feed node → limit to top 5 articles
3. **Loop with SplitInBatches**:
   o For each article:
      ▪ Use OpenAI:

      ```kotlin
      Summarize this article in 2-3 sentences.
      ```

4. **Collect Summaries**: Use Function or Merge node to combine
5. **Format Digest**:
   o Create a string with article titles + summaries
6. **Email Node**:
   o Subject: "Your Daily AI Digest – [Today's Date]"
   o Body: The combined summary

✅ **Done:** You've built a daily newsletter powered by AI summarization.

☐ Pro Tips for All Projects

Task	Tip
Parse structured OpenAI output	Use JSON format in prompt: `Return as JSON with keys: summary, tags...`

Task	Tip
Chain models efficiently	Add Delay nodes to prevent hitting API rate limits
Reuse prompts via Set nodes	Centralize prompts so they're easier to tweak
Monitor via logs	Log input/output pairs for audit and improvement
Test with edge cases	Try short, long, and unusual inputs during testing

✅ Recap

You've now walked through the **real-world solutions** to five end-to-end AI-powered workflows using:

- Hugging Face for classification and translation
- OpenAI for generation and summarization
- n8n's native nodes for logic, storage, and flow control

This final chapter gives you the foundation to **solve actual business problems** with smart automation — responsibly, efficiently, and creatively.

11.3 Ideas for Extending or Customizing Workflows

Now that you've built and tested real AI-powered workflows, it's time to **go beyond** the templates — and start thinking like a workflow architect. This section gives you practical ways to **extend**, **customize**, and **scale** your automation to fit different teams, tools, and use cases.

🔧 1. Add User Feedback Loops

💡 **Why: Improve AI performance over time.**

- Let users **rate the AI reply** (thumbs up/down, 1–5 stars)
- Store the rating alongside the original message and AI output
- Use this to **fine-tune prompts**, improve accuracy, or route poor responses to human review

✓ Can be done using a simple form input or email reply link.

☐ 2. Make Workflows Multilingual

💡 **Why: Serve users in more languages.**

- Detect language → Translate to English → Process → Translate reply back
- Store all three versions (original, internal, final)
- Add country/language to metadata for reporting

Use Hugging Face for translation or OpenAI with system prompts.

☐ 3. Use Embeddings for Smarter Memory (Advanced)

💡 **Why: Go beyond short-term memory with semantic search.**

- Store embeddings of past messages using OpenAI or Cohere
- Retrieve relevant past messages using cosine similarity
- Feed that context into the chatbot's prompt

Works great for FAQs, ongoing customer chats, or coaching bots.

⬇ 4. Add File Upload Support

💡 **Why: Enable richer input, like PDFs, CSVs, or screenshots.**

- Accept file via webhook, form, or email
- Use OCR or file parsers (PDF Parser, CSV Reader)
- Summarize, analyze, or extract data using OpenAI

✅ Example: "Summarize this uploaded contract" or "Extract top 5 bullet points from this CV."

☐ 5. Integrate with More Apps

💡 Why: Connect AI workflows to your real ecosystem.

Ideas:

- Save replies in Notion or Airtable
- Auto-create Jira tickets from urgent feedback
- Log AI summaries in your CRM
- Push product requests to Trello or Linear

Use n8n's **hundreds of built-in integrations** or HTTP requests.

☐☐ 6. Add Scheduled Batching

💡 Why: Process data in chunks at fixed times (for reports, summaries).

- Use a **Cron node** (e.g., daily at 5pm)
- Pull data from a Google Sheet or DB
- Loop through rows using `SplitInBatches`
- Summarize or tag in bulk
- Export via email or upload

Great for team reports, daily digests, or auto-tagging sessions.

🔔 7. Add Escalation Rules

💡 Why: Involve a human when AI is uncertain or fails.

- If confidence score < 0.6 → forward to Slack
- If OpenAI fails 3x → send backup message
- If summary mentions "urgent" or "legal" → send to legal team

✔️ Build failover logic using `If`, `Error Trigger`, and `Alert` nodes.

🎨 8. Customize Prompts Based on User Role or Use Case

💡 Why: Tailor AI tone and behavior.

- If user is a VIP → More detailed replies
- If internal vs external → Different formatting
- If topic = billing → Use formal tone; if feedback → Friendly tone

Use `Set` or `Function` nodes to dynamically modify prompts.

📊 9. Add Usage Reporting Dashboard

💡 Why: Track AI usage, costs, and outcomes.

Log and visualize:

- Number of AI calls per day
- Average prompt length
- Classification categories over time
- Error counts, retries

Use Google Sheets, Notion, or Supabase + dashboards like Retool or Metabase.

☐ 10. Fine-Tune AI Behavior via Prompt Engineering

💡 Why: Improve the quality of replies without changing the model.

Ideas:

- Add sample conversations in your prompt
- Give stricter instructions ("Be concise. Use bullet points.")
- Add role context: "You are a B2B support agent." or "You write SEO-friendly summaries."

✅ Recap

You can now take your AI workflows to the next level by:

- Adding feedback and memory
- Supporting more formats and languages
- Scaling to teams, CRMs, reports, or dashboards
- Making your bots smarter, faster, and more human-aware

These extensions turn n8n into **your own AI operations engine** — personalized, flexible, and production-ready.

Chapter 12: The Road Ahead

12.1 What's Next in AI + Automation

As you've seen throughout this book, combining **n8n** with **AI tools like OpenAI and Hugging Face** unlocks powerful new ways to automate tasks, improve decision-making, and personalize experiences.

But the field is just getting started. This final chapter explores where AI-powered automation is heading — and how you can stay ahead.

🚀 1. Multi-Agent Workflows Are Coming

Tools like **AutoGPT**, **CrewAI**, and **LangGraph** are leading the shift from **single-model AI use** to **multi-agent systems** — where multiple specialized agents collaborate to:

- Analyze data
- Perform research
- Make decisions
- Automate full workflows end-to-end

☞ *Imagine a support agent, a sentiment analyzer, and a business logic planner all working together inside your n8n flow.*

☐ 2. AI That Learns from Feedback (RAG & Fine-Tuning)

Right now, most workflows use **static prompts**. But the future is dynamic:

- **RAG (Retrieval-Augmented Generation)** will let AI answer based on *your company's data* — not just what it was trained on.
- **Fine-tuning** on company tone, FAQs, or user interactions will make bots more accurate and on-brand.

🎯 This means *smarter, faster, and more personalized automation at scale.*

☐ 3. Visual Workflow Builders Will Dominate AI Ops

As AI gets more powerful, **low-code platforms like n8n** will become the home base for:

- Prompt engineering
- Agent orchestration
- AI observability
- Secure, explainable pipelines

🎯 *n8n becomes your AI command center.*

☐ 4. AI + APIs = New Forms of Work

Many teams are moving from **manual tasks** to:

- Smart assistants for internal ops
- AI-driven customer service bots
- Auto-generated reports, posts, and replies
- AI agents that schedule, respond, and act

🎯 *You're not just automating tasks — you're redesigning how work gets done.*

☐ 5. Developer-Friendly AI Will Explode

Expect better tools for:

- Debugging prompts

- Tracking usage + latency
- Building AI "apps" in workflows
- Combining multiple LLM providers (e.g., OpenAI + Claude)

☞ *You'll be able to mix, test, and optimize AI models as easily as choosing HTTP endpoints.*

🔐 6. Trust, Safety, and Transparency Will Be Non-Negotiable

As AI gets more involved in decision-making, you'll need to:

- Log every AI output
- Flag when AI is used
- Review low-confidence responses
- Store feedback for future tuning

☞ *Responsible AI workflows = future-proof AI workflows.*

✅ What You Can Do Next

Step	Why It Matters
💡 Keep experimenting	New nodes, models, and plugins are released fast
🏛 Build real use cases	Content tools, internal bots, client projects
☐ Revisit your workflows	Improve prompts, add memory, or speed up logic
☐ Learn RAG or fine-tuning	Adapt models to your domain
☐ Share your builds	Inspire others and improve via feedback

☐ Final Thought

AI isn't just a feature — it's a **new layer of intelligence** for your entire stack.
With n8n, you're not just using AI — you're **orchestrating it**.

You now have the foundation to build smart, safe, scalable automation with AI at the core.
Keep building, keep testing, and don't be afraid to push boundaries.

12.2 Staying Up-to-Date with n8n and Model Improvements

AI and automation move fast — and what works today may be outdated in a few months. To build workflows that remain **relevant, efficient, and cutting-edge**, you'll need to stay plugged into both the **n8n ecosystem** and **AI model advancements**.

Here's how to keep your skills sharp and your automations future-proof.

☐ Why Staying Updated Matters

Area	What Changes Frequently	Why It Matters
n8n Features	New nodes, triggers, integrations	Easier automation, new capabilities
API Providers	Rate limits, endpoints, key formats	Prevent workflow breakage
AI Models	New versions (e.g., GPT-4, Claude 3)	Better performance, cost-efficiency, capabilities
Security	Credential handling, data privacy updates	Keeps workflows safe and compliant

---

☐ 1. Follow n8n Release Notes

n8n releases new versions **almost weekly** with new nodes, bug fixes, and improvements.

- 📌 n8n Release Log
- ☐☐ Watch for:
    - New nodes (AI, email, messaging, dev tools)
    - Node improvements (e.g., OpenAI system message support)
    - Credential handling changes
    - Community-contributed integrations

✅ Tip: Bookmark the n8n GitHub Repo and star it for updates.

☐ 2. Track AI Model Updates

AI providers like **OpenAI**, **Hugging Face**, and **Anthropic** release:

- New model versions
- Pricing changes
- Rate limits or deprecation notices

🔎 Stay tuned to:

- OpenAI changelog
- Hugging Face model hub
- Claude/Anthropic

✅ Tip: Always specify model versions explicitly in prompts to avoid unexpected behavior.

📡 3. Join the Community

🔗 n8n Community Channels:

- n8n Community Forum
- Discord server
- GitHub Discussions

Ask questions, discover AI templates, and share your use cases.

☐ AI + Automation Resources:

- LangChain
- OpenAI Cookbook
- Papers with Code
- AI newsletters like *The Rundown* or *Ben's Bites*

✅ Follow AI researchers, builders, and product teams on X (Twitter) and LinkedIn.

☐ 4. Test New Models with Drop-in Swaps

n8n makes it easy to:

- Swap OpenAI → Claude or Hugging Face
- Try LLaMA, Mistral, or custom hosted models via HTTP node
- Benchmark quality, latency, and token costs

🎯 Set up **parallel AI calls** for A/B testing and choose the best performer.

📅 5. Revisit and Refactor Workflows

Every few months:

- Review prompts for clarity and performance
- Add retry logic or fallbacks to new nodes
- Replace brittle API calls with newer or more stable ones
- Optimize for cost and speed

✅ Your workflows are living systems — treat them like products.

✅ Recap: Staying Up-to-Date Checklist

Task	Frequency
Check n8n changelog	Weekly
Review AI model updates & pricing	Monthly
Join forums + communities	Ongoing
Re-test and optimize key workflows	Quarterly
Backup + export your key automations	Monthly

🎯 Final Advice

The AI + automation space is evolving rapidly — but staying current doesn't mean constant change.
Build a system that adapts, not one that depends on static tools.

With n8n, you now have a platform that evolves with you — and the skills to stay one step ahead.